IDENTITY

Who We Are

Troll Target Series

TROLL TARGET SERIES

Lewis Gardner	*Senior Editor*
Miriam Rinn	*Editor*
Virginia Pass	*Teaching Guides*
Cris Peterson	*Bibliographies*
Peter Pluchino	*Cover Illustration*

PROJECT CONSULTANT

David Dillon *Professor of Language Arts, McGill University, Montreal*

ACKNOWLEDGEMENTS

"A List of 10 Things" first appeared in *Merlyn's Pen:The National Magazines of Student Writing*. Reprinted with permission of Merlyn's Pen; E. Greenwich, RI 02818

"A Man's Heart May Be in His Environment, But Heredity Is Where He Got His Nose. . . ." reprinted with the permission of Simon & Schuster from *Half the Battle* by Bill Vaughan. Copyright © 1967 by Bill Vaughan.

(Acknowledgements continued on page 159)

Printed in the United States of America.   ISBN 0-8167-4276-6

10 9 8 7 6 5 4 3 2 1

Contents

A List of 10 Things

by Loubel Cruz

We all need a list of things to remember—to help us keep in mind who we are and what is important to us. Loubel Cruz was a high school student when she wrote this story about a major disruption in a teenager's life.

There is a window right next to my seat in sixth-period literature that offers a view of the courtyard. Good thing, that window, for if it wasn't there, I would be asleep. I listened restlessly to Sister Mary Catherine lecture on and on about who the main characters were in *A Tale of Two Cities.* I watched the snow gently falling on the statue of St. Francis of Assisi, the patron saint after whom my school was named, amazed at how much snow had already accumulated. It was the beginning of February, and, being a native Texan, I was not used to foot-deep snow packs on my sidewalk every morning. But that's what you get when you move to Boston—home of the Red Sox, commercial fishing, and blizzards. I smiled at that thought, for it was exactly what Davis warned me about before I moved here, except he probably didn't know how right he was. I laughed inside when I thought of Davis. Then my heart began to hurt when I thought about how the move here was the most difficult thing I'd ever done. It all started about five months ago. Five months ago when the biggest event in my short, but unpredictable, 15 years began.

It was a hot, humid day in October. The kind of day you wish the air conditioner was going full blast and that there was more ice in your lemonade and that you'd put on more deodorant that morning. I was living in Houston, Texas, where I'd lived all my life, and attended Duke Senior High, where I was a freshman.

"My parents are acting weird, all secretive and stuff," I told Davis Vaughn. It was worrying me, it really was.

We were sitting in my room after school and Davis was checking, or should I say copying, my geometry answers. He didn't like math, and never really tried at it. His favorite subject was gym. Davis was convinced he was going to become all-pro in every sport that ever existed and become a "kabillionaire." And even though he taunted me about my dream, which was to become a writer, I never once thought of shattering his hopes.

"Look, Marshall, everything will be okay. Your parents have just been hanging around mine too much. It makes them wacko too," Davis said, not taking his eyes off the postulates and theorems.

A couple of years ago he came up with this wonderful idea to call me by my last name—which is Marshall—instead of my first—which is Colleen. He said Colleen was too feminine. I said I was a girl. He said he wasn't sure. I said for him to stuff it. It was all annoying at first, but I got used to it.

Davis Vaughn is my best friend. I never really told him that, and now that I think of it, I never admitted it to anyone else; I bet he never has either. But we knew. We knew deep down and our friendship was so strong we didn't have to say it.

"Well, I'd better be going home now," Davis said, closing the geometry book. "It's broccoli quiche night. Don't worry, Marshall, everything will be cool."

I looked at him, storm clouds in my eyes.

"I promise." He smiled at me, his eyes sparkling. The "Davis sparkle," as I called it.

That night at dinner, I played with my food, occasionally forcing a small piece of lasagna down my throat. My parents kept looking at me funny, very curious about what my problem was. Good, that's what I wanted; I wanted to know what was wrong, too.

"Colleen, sweetie, is anything wrong?" my mom asked, putting more food on my plate, pretending not to notice the unfinished pieces that were still there.

I shook my head.

My parents exchanged worried glances and then, after a while, my father spoke. "Collie, there's something we have been wanting to tell you."

I swallowed hard. Oh no, here it comes! I thought of every bad thing that could have happened.

"We're moving."

"Huh?" I knew what he said; I just wanted to pretend he didn't say it, hoping I was wrong. Funny, that wasn't one of the things I thought he might say.

My father looked at my mom nervously and then looked at me, forcing a weak smile. "Bennett and Foresman have opened up a new firm in Boston. And, well . . . they picked me to manage it. Collie, it's the chance of a lifetime, one that I've been waiting for."

I stared. Not at my parents, but down, at my hands. Davis once said, jokingly, that I had beautiful hands. But in a way, I thought he meant it. My hands were sweating now. They were nervous. Davis would have been disappointed.

"Collie?" my mom said, concerned. "It's going to be great, sweetie, I promise. There will be lots of snow. You always loved snow." She was talking to me as if I was a two-year-old. It must have been already determined.

After a couple of unbearable minutes of silence, I opened my mouth but nothing came out. Finally a voice whispered, "Boston? When?"

"We want to have you ready for the second semester, so we want to move during Christmas vacation."

I don't remember who answered me, and I don't remember starting to cry, either. I do recall my mom handing me a pink Kleenex which I refused to accept, and the strained expression on my father's face, as if he'd just ruined my adolescence forever.

"Uh, Mom, I have some homework. Could I . . . ."

"Sure, sweetie, go ahead."

7

I walked slowly to my room and closed the door behind me. Almost instinctively, I picked up the phone by my bed and waited for the person on the other end to make my tears stop.

"Hello?"

"Hello, Davis?"

"Marshall? Hey, what's up?"

I didn't answer. I was thinking.

"Marshall? Everything okay? Marrshhaall!"

"Yeah, everything's cool." I couldn't tell him. I was depressed . . . and scared. "Just wanted to know if you had a game tomorrow."

"Yup. Playing King Memorial. We're gonna get creamed." I already knew that.

"Okay, I was just wondering. Bye."

"Later."

I got up and began to pace. I didn't know how to feel, act, or what to say. It really started to tick me off. I felt a tear form in my eye and quickly brushed it away. When I start to cry, I never can stop. But those stupid tears kept forming, multiplying by the second. They fell down my face, leaving black streaks of mascara under my eyes. Then the crying turned into sobs, deep hard chokes that could not be controlled. I fell onto my bed, buried my head in the pillow, and, still crying, fell asleep.

The next afternoon found Davis and me in my room, engaged in our daily ritual of me doing geometry and Davis copying it. The day had been terrible. I spent most of it trying to avoid my friends and trying not to cry. Davis knew something was wrong, but was smart enough not to ask what it was. I knew I had to tell him, though.

"I'm moving."

"Hmmmm?" He was too caught up in trying to get the altitude length of a right triangle.

"I'm moving."

"Yeah, right."

"Davis," I said angrily, reaching over the bed and slamming the geometry book closed. "I'm serious."

Davis looked at me hard, straight into my eyes. After what seemed an eternity, he looked down. He knew the truth.

"Where?"

"Boston."

"When?"

"Christmas vacation."

Finally his eyes met mine. The "Davis sparkle" wasn't in them. "Why?"

I started to feel my heart knot. "It's not my decision."

Davis looked down and pretended to be engrossed in the design of my bedspread. He said nothing, but I knew exactly how he felt. Finally, without looking up, he spoke.

"Boston's pretty cool, I guess, the Red Sox and all. There's gonna be a lot of snow. You can ice-skate a lot." He picked up the geometry book and continued to study.

"Geez, Davis, you sound like my mother." I was getting angry now. He acted like he didn't care.

"Well, geez, Colleen, what do you want me to say? That I'm really glad you're moving so I can hang out with Herman Waltflower? I can't say what I want. I can't say don't go because I know you have to." There was anger and confusion in his eyes. I had never seen him this way. It scared me—he called me Colleen.

"It's not my fault," I said, the tears starting to flow.

"Look, I gotta go now. It's getting late." Davis got up, gathered his things, and without another word, left, slamming the door behind him.

I didn't cry that night. I was too mad—at everybody. At my dad for accepting a job thousands of miles away, at my mom for agreeing to go along with it, at Davis for being such a lousy friend when I needed him most, and at me for being mad and not crying.

The next day I tried to find Davis to talk to him, but at the same time tried to avoid his presence. The first time I saw him was in Mrs. Drew's English class. He didn't look my way, so I tried not to look his. We were studying poetry, and our assignment for the day was to write a list of 10 things. God only knows how that is poetry, but I was too preoccupied to think about it. I looked over at Davis to see if he would give me one of his this-is-such-a-stupid-class looks, but he didn't. He just stared straight ahead, very intent on what Mrs. Drew was saying. He didn't talk to me for the rest of the school day.

That afternoon the doorbell rang. I was too busy lying on my bed being depressed to answer it, but then I remembered no one was home. I lazily opened the door.

9

"Could you help me with geometry? I have no idea what's going on." Davis gave me a shy grin and invited himself inside.

"Davis, I'm sorry. I really shouldn't have . . . ."

"Hey, Marshall, forget about it. It's not your fault. I should be the one who's sorry. Boston, huh? No offense, but you're gonna freeze your rear up there."

I laughed. This was the way it should have been.

"Let's not talk about you moving anymore, okay? Promise?"

"Promise."

Davis smiled, satisfied. "So what did you think about Drew's poem today? I wrote 10 reasons why the Oilers never made it to the Super Bowl. What a stupid class."

And that was that.

Two months came and went. And as we promised, Davis and I didn't mention anything about moving. He helped me pack, but we never actually discussed why. We went on with our daily routine as if I wasn't leaving: him copying geometry, me watching his football games, him proofreading my newspaper articles.

Then the day before moving day came. We were in my room comparing Christmas presents. We laughed, talked, and gossiped, but we knew the time to say goodbye was coming nearer.

"Uh, well, Merry Christmas," he said, giving me a small wrapped box.

"Thanks," I said, opening the gift. I already gave him my present that morning, which I don't think he really liked—but he did a really good job of acting like he did.

Inside the box was a golden locket. It was beautiful.

"Uh, my mom picked it out because you know how I am with girl presents," he said, laughing. "I thought you would like it, though. I didn't put my picture in it 'cause you might find a really cute guy up there in Massachusetts. But there's something engraved in it so you won't forget me."

"Thanks." I immediately put it on. I loved it.

"Oh, here's another thing." He gave me a small envelope. He smiled. "This is really from me. Don't open it yet, though. After I leave."

I wanted to ask why, but I just nodded obediently.

"Well, I gotta go now. It's getting late." He got up awkwardly and headed for the door. "Boston will be awesome, Marshall. I promise.

You'll be fine." He smiled at me.

"Bye."

"Later." Davis opened my bedroom door.

I felt tears running down my face. "I love you, Davis."

He turned around and smiled. His eyes sparkled with little tear-drops ready to fall. "I know, Marshall." And with that he walked away.

I closed my door and let the dam break. I sat down on the floor, and through the tears read what Davis had written.

TEN THINGS COLLEEN K. MARSHALL
SHOULD ALWAYS REMEMBER IN BOSTON
1. Don't get one of those gross New England accents.
2. In association with #1, say "y'all" as much as possible.
3. She's beautiful.
4. Even if she's in Boston, she will always be a Texan at heart.
5. Her name is Marshall.
6. No matter what anyone tells her, she's going to be a writer. She will write only the truth.
7. It's not her fault if a certain person flunks geometry. Ha, ha.
8. She's not fat, she's not fat, she's not fat.
9. Oilers rule!
10. And the last thing Colleen K. Marshall should always remember in Boston is that even though he never says it, Davis R. Vaughn loves her too.

How could he write this? He knew I would cry. Despite all my tears, I found myself laughing. Laughing at what he wrote and all the good times we had. Davis knew me so well, better than anyone else, and I was leaving him. But as the gold locket said, "We'll always be together."

So here I am in Boston, going to a Catholic private school (thank heaven it's coed), wearing a red plaid uniform I wouldn't be caught dead wearing in Houston, and shoveling snow from my driveway every morning.

The bell rang. I slowly gathered my things from Sister Mary Catherine's literature class and walked out the door. I hadn't made many friends here—well, I really hadn't tried that hard—so it surprised me when I heard someone call my name down the hallway.

I turned and saw a guy running toward me, panting.

"Hi, I'm Richard Luis. I'm the editor of the newspaper here. Call me Rick, though."

"Oh, hi. I'm Colleen Marshall. Call me . . . ." I thought about it, "Colleen."

"I know." I felt surprised and kind of flattered that he did. "Sister Agnes says you're a very talented writer. We heard that you were on the news staff at your old school . . . in Texas?"

"Yes I was, in Houston."

"Houston, huh? The Oilers are pretty good."

I smiled, choking back a giggle.

"Well, anyway," he continued, "we really need some good writers, so I was wondering if you'd like to be on the staff."

"Yeah, that would be great." I couldn't believe my luck.

"Cool. What do you write?"

I thought of the list of 10 things, which reminded me of Davis. "Only the truth."

A Man's Heart May Be in His Environment, But Heredity Is Where He Got His Nose....

by Bill Vaughan

Many people think that their identities are strongly influenced by their appearance and their heredity. Humorist Bill Vaughan takes a lighthearted look at these serious topics.

The changing of the calendar reminds us of the passage of time and produces a lot of writing in which people address themselves either to posterity or the past. I hesitate to speak to posterity, as they are a crowd I have never run with and I don't know whether they will be my type or not. So I thought that what I might do is drop a note of thanks to my ancestors.

I want to thank them for this big nose they gave me.

I am not a geneticist, but I know that if you want a blue-eyed fruit fly you have to be pretty particular about which fruit fly marries which. It's not just a matter of one fruit fly saying he is in love with the girl next door. You've got to check on her family and be sure that the genes and chromosomes are all blue.

Or take basketball players. They have to be planned to grow that tall.

13

Which is the way it is with my nose. Somewhere back in a Welsh coal pit, where the whole thing began, my ancestors had to decide whether to go in for height or noses. They opted nasally. Of course, this was long before basketball was invented and they didn't know that being 6 feet, 8 inches tall would be an advantage some day. All they knew was that it would be a pain in the neck while mining coal.

So down the centuries they have always aimed toward the Ultimate Nose. There were times when somebody might have fallen in love with a rich girl. But my ancestors never did because, apparently, the rich girls had snub noses.

The people in my family always had an instinct for the nose. They went for it, and I can only hope that the result has made them happy.

In all modesty I have to say that when someone sits down to compile a list of the 10 Great Noses of History, I will be among them. I won't rank myself, but I am right up there with Cyrano de Bergerac and Charles de Gaulle, and maybe I'm number one, because the first is fictional and the second may be also.

We don't count Jimmy Durante because he has commercialized his nose. It is a popular success and has been written up in the news magazines, which means that it is out as far as true nose connoisseurs are concerned.

As I say, when my ancestors started out on noses they had never heard of basketball any more than anybody else had, so they couldn't have known that if they had reached for height I might be 7 feet tall and have gotten my college education free. There are no scholarships for noses.

But I am far from complaining. If you are a big, tall gawk, nobody notices you. It has been drummed into everybody that tall people don't like to be asked how is the weather up there and other overworked questions. They have learned not to say to a tall person, "Pardon me if my breath is fogging your belt buckle."

The tall person is ignored because we have discovered from reading countless interviews with basketball players that they want to be treated just like anyone else. You will often see a tall person standing alone at a party. Not so the man with a really big nose.

He is surrounded by a chatty group saying witticisms such as, "Is that your nose, or are you playing the piccolo?" or, "Well, one good thing, you can smoke a cigar in the rain."

Show me the center of hilarity and laughter, with the pretty girls and the more substantial community leaders, and I will show you a man with a big nose.

Unfortunately, some parents are so devoted to impressing upon their children that they should not comment upon physical characteristics that they overdo. They say, "Now, when you meet Mr. Vaughan, whatever you do, don't comment upon the size of his nose."

I can always tell when a child has had this point hammered home. He shakes hands politely and says, "How do you do, Mr. Nose."

These parents should realize that my nose is my only claim to distinction. I like to have it mentioned, and it usually is. I don't know how millionaires feel, but I know if I were one I would be disappointed if nobody talked about my money.

Perhaps the analogy is bad. Anybody can have money. If my ancestors had gone in for money or good looks, where would I be today? Just another handsome rich man. Nobody would notice me twice. But with a nose like this they notice me three or four times.

Unwanted

by Edward Field

The poster with my picture on it
Is hanging on the bulletin board in the Post Office.

I stand by it hoping to be recognized
Posing first full face and then profile

But everyone passes by and I have to admit
The photograph was taken some years ago.

I was unwanted then and I'm unwanted now
Ah guess ah'll go up echo mountain and crah.

I wish someone would find my fingerprints somewhere
Maybe on a corpse and say, You're it.

Description: Male, or reasonably so
Complexion white, but not lily-white

Thirty-fivish, and looks it lately
Five-feet-nine and one-hundred-thirty pounds: no physique

Black hair going gray, hairline receding fast
What used to be curly, now fuzzy

Brown eyes starey under beetling brow
Mole on chin, probably will become a wen

It is perfectly obvious that he was not popular at school
No good at baseball, and wet his bed.

His aliases tell his history: Dumbbell, Good-for-nothing,
Jewboy, Fieldinsky, Skinny, Fierce Face, Greaseball, Sissy.

Warning: This man is not dangerous, answers to any name
Responds to love, don't call him or he will come.

16

Hum It Again, Jeremy

by Jean Davies Okimoto

Who we are and how we live may begin with our families, but as teenager Jeremy Botkin learns in this play, sometimes we're on our own.

CHARACTERS

JEREMY BOTKIN, *a young man about 16*
ROSALIE BOTKIN, *his mother*
DAN BOTKIN, *his father*
DARRELL WASHINGTON, *Jeremy's best friend*

SETTING

TIME: *An evening in May.*
PLACE: *Cleveland, Ohio.*

An asphalt basketball court on a dimly lit playground, center stage, in front of an apartment building. It is littered with cans and papers. There is one streetlight above the hoop. As the curtain rises, we see DARRELL WASHINGTON, *a 16-year-old young man dressed in jeans and a T-shirt, shooting baskets alone on the court. It is eight o'clock.*

DARRELL: Where have you been, man?

> [*Irritated, he pivots and makes a sharp chest shot to* JEREMY BOTKIN, *who bursts on the court, out of breath. He is a tall, gangly 16-year-old, dressed in jeans and a Cleveland Cavaliers T-shirt.*]

JEREMY [*catches ball, jarred backward a bit by its unexpected force. He tucks ball under his arm and makes "time out" signal*]: Time.

> [*He throws ball underarm like a referee to* DARRELL.]

DARRELL [*accusingly*]: It's dark.

JEREMY [*holding hands up, shaking his head*]: Not you too—I can't handle it.

DARRELL [*pauses, irritated. He looks around the court, dribbling the ball hard. Then sighs, resignedly*]: Okay. [*He bounces the ball once, catches it, and pauses again.*] Let's play.

JEREMY [*guarding* DARRELL, *who dribbles toward basket*]: Thanks for waiting. [DARRELL *shoots, guarded by* JEREMY, *then* JEREMY *shoots, guarded by* DARRELL. DARRELL *shoots, guarded by* JEREMY.]: Nice shot. [*Substitute* "Almost . . . nice shot" *if ball doesn't go in.*]

DARRELL [*guarding* JEREMY, *who takes shot*]: I figured it was your mom, your old man, or Renee.

JEREMY: All of the above.

> [*Guards* DARRELL, *who shoots. He gets* DARRELL'*s rebound, then shoots and misses, and* DARRELL *gets the ball.*]

DARRELL: It's the Jam Man.

> [*Dribbles to basket, goes up, and slam dunks in the air a foot below the basket.* JEREMY *cracks up at the air dunk.* DARRELL *passes to* JEREMY.]

JEREMY [*dribbling toward basket as* DARRELL *guards*]: You know what would be great?

DARRELL [*guarding* JEREMY]: What?

JEREMY [*shoots, catches his own rebound, and dribbles ball in place*]: If you could do a trade. In your family—like it was a team. I'd get a power father. My present one doesn't come to play—as they say. [*Passes ball to* DARRELL] So I'd just trade him.

DARRELL [*dribbling toward basket as* JEREMY *guards*]: For money? Or another player?

18

JEREMY: My mom would want the money. She's into the green. It's all she talks about, but this is my deal, see? I'd trade him for another player. [*Shooting*] I'd trade him for Bill Cosby.

DARRELL [*shouting excitedly*]: All right! My mom for Tina Turner!

JEREMY [*bending down to tie his shoe*]: That's not the idea, man. You never see Tina Turner with kids or anything like that. See—you scout a different kind of talent for this trade. Like, take Bill Cosby. Everyone knows he loved his kids—

DARRELL [*holding ball, snapping fingers and singing Tina Turner song*]: "What's love got to do, got to do with it?"

JEREMY [*stands up, takes ball from* DARRELL. *Flatly*]: Sometimes—I wonder.

> [*Dribbles toward basket. Freezes as set becomes black.*]
> *Earlier the same day.*
> *Spots light the living room of the Botkin apartment, which is set on risers on the left of the stage. Furnished with a worn couch and matching chair, it is a small L-shaped room with a formica dinette set in the end of the room next to the adjoining small kitchen, which is offstage. On an end table next to the chair is a phone with a long extension cord that can reach around the corner to the kitchen offstage. An exercise bike is in the corner of the room facing a television set. Over the television is a macramé wall hanging, and on the wall behind the dinette set is a plate commemorating the wedding of Prince Charles and Princess Di. There is a large plant in the corner of the living room, many of its leaves brown and dying. On the formica coffee table in front of the sofa is an arrangement of plastic flowers and a Walkman radio.* ROSALIE BOTKIN *is riding the exercise bike and watching the shopping channel on TV. She is a short, chunky woman with obviously dyed auburn hair. Dressed in pink sweats, she is scowling and puffing as she pedals the bike.*

ROSALIE [*shouting*]: Jeremy! Don't leave this apartment without talking to me. [*She pedals laboriously and begins to pant before shouting again, louder.*] I have to talk to you, Jeremy.

> [JEREMY *enters, leans against top of easy chair, holding car keys.*]

JEREMY: I gotta go, Mom. After I have dinner with him—I'm supposed to meet Darrell. [*Heads for the door.*]

ROSALIE: Just tell him to give me the check. [*She runs a hand through her hair, then wipes her forearm across her brow.*] I want that check, Jeremy. [*Carefully, she gets off the bike, rubbing her thighs, then slowly goes to the chair and flops down in it as the phone rings.*] Stay right here—I'm not through. [*While* ROSALIE *answers the phone,* JEREMY *dribbles and shoots an imaginary basketball.*] Hello . . . .Yeah, he's here. [*Covering the mouthpiece*] It's that girl. Why don't you bring her to meet me? She's forward enough to call you, she ought to meet your mother. [*She hands the phone to* JEREMY.] Here.

JEREMY [*taking the phone, angrily mouthing*]: Shhhhhh.

   [*He disappears into the kitchen around the corner with the phone.*]

ROSALIE [*nagging, as* JEREMY *disappears to kitchen*]: And if you want to know, I still don't think it's right for girls to be calling boys. [*She lies on the floor, begins doing sit-ups; after four sit-ups* JEREMY *enters and heads for door. She sits up.*] You were the one card I had, Jeremy. If he didn't pay—I wouldn't let him see you. So—now you're driving a car, you're a big guy, you go see the jerk whenever you please. You think we don't need the money or something? Don't you give a damn about my feelings?

JEREMY [*impatiently, jiggling the car keys*]: Listen Mom—

ROSALIE: No, you listen! Because of you I don't have any control over this situation. Not unless I want to go to some lawyer, and those greedy slobs won't even talk to me unless I give 'em a hundred bucks up front. Now if I had an extra hundred bucks lying around, I wouldn't need a lawyer, would I?

JEREMY [*nodding, defeatedly*]: Yeah, Mom. [*Quietly, mumbling*] Yeah.

ROSALIE [*softening*]: Look, this is strictly business. Why can't you see that you're the only leverage I've got? I'm not trying to make you hate him, Jeremy.

JEREMY: You know . . . . [*He pauses, leaning back against door.*] It's beyond me how the two of you ever got together.

ROSALIE [*quietly, shaking her head*]: You aren't the only one to wonder that.

JEREMY: What d'you mean, Mom?

ROSALIE [*stands and gets on exercise bike*]: Oh—just that no one ever looked at me. I was just known as Elaine's kid sister. [*starts pedaling*] So when Dan Botkin came around for me, I thought it was a mistake. And then—when he actually wanted to marry me—me, Rosalie—well.... [*She pauses.*] I thought I'd died and gone to heaven.

JEREMY: Some heaven.

ROSALIE [*bitterly*]: Yeah. Some heaven. I shoulda known better. Like ya been told, your grandfather was a drunk—just as well you didn't know that bum—but your father didn't touch the stuff—and that impressed me. In fact, I thought I was the luckiest girl on the block. [*sighs*] But for all the good he did us, he might as well've been a drunk like his old man. Dan's great disappearing act. Now you see him—now you don't. When I think about it, the only thing he ever did for me [*Pausing*] was for one brief moment in my life [*Pausing again, leaning forward on handlebars*] he made me feel beautiful. [*She shakes her head, starts pedaling.*] I guess that's something.

JEREMY [*embarrassed*]: I gotta go, Mom.

ROSALIE [*fiercely*]: Jeremy, you tell your father that if he doesn't come up with that check, I got a lawyer who'll call his lines and garnish his pay. You tell him that, Jeremy!

JEREMY: See you later, Mom. [*Turns toward door.*]

ROSALIE [*stops pedaling. Tenderly, as* JEREMY *exits*]: Drive carefully, Jeremy. [*Gets off bike, goes to door and shouts after him.*] Jeremy! You damn well better come back here with that check!

> *Set becomes black.*
>
> *Lights come back up on basketball court.* JEREMY *and* DARRELL *are sitting on the ground leaning back against the apartment wall that borders the court.*

JEREMY: You see the Cavs last night?

DARRELL: A little, before I had to go to work. They didn't look that bad in the first quarter.

JEREMY: They sure blew it in the fourth. It was pitiful. I shoulda gone over to Renee's instead of watching 'em. I oughta give up on those clowns.

DARRELL: How's Renee?

JEREMY [*depressed*]: Mr. Sanduzi wouldn't let me see her.

DARRELL: That's cold.

21

JEREMY [*sarcastically*]: Yeah. Tell me about it. [*He stands and bounces the ball.*] I stop by her apartment on my way to see my dad. She'd even called and asked me to come by. So I get there, I buzz their apartment, and Mr. Sanduzi comes on the intercom. He says [*mimicking a low growling voice*] "Renee's got to help her mother, Botkin. Don't come up here."

> [*He passes the ball to* DARRELL, *who stands in place and dribbles it.* JEREMY *picks up a can and throws it against the brick wall of the apartment building.*]

DARRELL: It was bad with your dad too—huh?

JEREMY: Yeah. Like I said—he doesn't come to play.

> *Set darkens.*
>
> *Earlier that evening:*
>
> *Spots light* DAN BOTKIN's *apartment bedroom, which is set on risers on the right of stage. It is furnished with a double bed, a dresser, a chair, and an end table that holds a phone and a lamp. A closet is across from the bed; next to the chair is a window. The furnishings are sparse and cheap in contrast to the appearance of* DAN BOTKIN, *a balding, middle-aged man; he is a sharp dresser, wearing a silk sport coat. He has several large gold rings on his fingers.* DAN *is packing his suitcase while* JEREMY *stands by the window, looking out.*

DAN [*cheerily*]: Who d'ya think'll make the playoffs, Jeremy?

JEREMY [*looking out the window, turning away from* DAN]: I dunno.

DAN: Sonics are looking good.

JEREMY [*sadly*]: Yeah.

DAN: Bullets have a shot. [*chuckles*] Little joke there, Jeremy. [*He pauses, waiting for a response from* JEREMY, *who silently stares out the window.*] Hey—not even a courtesy laugh?

JEREMY: I don't feel like laughing.

DAN: Look—I told you I was sorry about tonight. We'll do it some other time.

JEREMY [*mumbling, voice fading*]: Like always—

DAN: What? Speak up, wouldya?

JEREMY [*shouting*]: It's always some other time!

DAN: Listen, kid. You don't have it so bad. Name one time I ever laid a hand on you, Jeremy.

JEREMY [*expressionless*]: You never laid a hand on me, Dad.

DAN: See this watch? Read that name. R-O-L-E-X. Best watch money can buy, and I earned every damn dime to pay for it. My old man couldn't blink at a watch like this. You know, Jeremy—when I wear this watch [*Pausing*] I feel like somebody. It's insurance, too. I've never had to—but if I ever got in a jam—it's liquid—instant cash. But so far [*Knocking on dresser*] the Lord willin' and the river don't rise—I've never had to.

JEREMY [*coldly*]: Mom says she needs the check.

DAN [*defensively*]: Look, Jeremy, my lines aren't paying me. They're slime. Take it from me, don't ever be a rep in the rag business—it's not worth it. They're supposed to pay me next week. [*Angrily, slamming suitcase shut*] Tell your mother I'm doing the best I can.

JEREMY: When'll you be back?

DAN: This week I've got Akron, Salem, Columbus, and Cincinnati. Probably the end of the week—but I know a gal in Cincinnati, so— might be the first of next if I get lucky. She's pretty—but I got my eyes open. You can't trust pretty women. You want one that'll stick around. I'm sure what led my old man to the bottle was when my mother took off. [*Lifts suitcase off bed.*] You know, the only thing I remember about her is bright-red lips and she smelled like cigarettes and soap. Funny, huh?

JEREMY: Yeah.

DAN: And a little song she used to sing. Only you know what, Jeremy?

JEREMY [*sadly*]: What?

DAN: I even forgot the song. [*Gets trench coat from the closet.*] So— tell your mother—next week. [*Takes out wallet and hands Jeremy a five-dollar bill.*] Sorry about dinner. Get yourself something to eat with this, okay?

JEREMY [*taking bill, looking at floor*]: Can I see you next week?

DAN: Sure, kid—I'll call you.

> *Set become black.*
>
> *Scenes alternate among the basketball court,* JEREMY's *apartment, and* DAN BOTKIN's *apartment.*

JEREMY [*holding ball under his arm*]: Beats me why I don't give up on the jerk.

DARRELL [*shrugging*]: Maybe for the same reason we don't give up on the Cavs.

JEREMY: Yeah. Every season we think this'll be the year they put it all together. [*Pauses*] You know—sometimes I feel like this damn ball.

[*Bounces ball four times. Set becomes black. Spot on stage left.*]

ROSALIE [*rapidly*]: Tell your father—

[*Ball bounces once, punctuating. Spot on stage right.*]

DAN: Tell your mother—

[*Ball bounces once. Spot on stage left.*]

ROSALIE: Tell your father—

[*Ball bounces once. Spot on stage right.*]

DAN: Tell your mother—

[*Ball bounces once. Spot on stage left.*]

ROSALIE: Tell your father—

[*Ball bounces once. Spot on stage right.*]

DAN: Tell your mother—

[*Ball bounces once. Set darkens. Spot on basketball court.*]

DARRELL [*dribbling toward basket as* JEREMY *guards*]: Who was the greatest forward?

JEREMY [*going up for rebound and getting it*]: All-time?

DARRELL [*guarding* JEREMY]: All-time.

JEREMY [*shooting*]: Elgin Baylor.

DARRELL [*getting rebound as* JEREMY *guards him*]: The Bird Man.

JEREMY [*catches ball that* DARRELL *passes to him. They pass it back and forth, taking a break from the game*]: The greatest guard?

DARRELL: Magic.

JEREMY: Michael Jordan.

DARRELL: Jerry West.

JEREMY: Oscar Robertson.

DARRELL: Gail Goodrich. [*Dribbles toward basket and shoots, as* JEREMY *guards.*]

JEREMY [*getting rebound, takes ball out and shoots, while* DARRELL *guards*]: Center?

DARRELL [*Bounce passes to* JEREMY, *who returns it as they punctuate each player they name with a pass*]: Kareem.

JEREMY: Bill Russell.

DARRELL: Wilt Chamberlain.

JEREMY: Akeem Olajuwon.

DARRELL: Soon to be the greatest?

JEREMY: Mark Eaton. [*Dribbles the ball toward basket. Stops. There* *is a pause as he holds ball and looks straight at* DARRELL.] Know who I'd like to be?

DARRELL [*standing under basket, leaning against pole*]: Who, man?

JEREMY [*quietly*]: Denny.

DARRELL: Denny? Who—Denny Crum? Coach at Louisville?

JEREMY [*bounces ball once, then holds it again*]: Nope.

DARRELL: You mean baseball? That Tigers pitcher Denny McClain?

JEREMY [*walks across court and sits down, leaning back against the brick wall of the apartment building*]: Denny. The guy that owns all those restaurants. Makes people happy. You know, Denny's. It's open all night. All day. You can get pancakes and stuff—everybody likes to go there. That Denny.

DARRELL [*walks to edge of court.* JEREMY *tosses him the ball. He sits down next to* JEREMY]: Yeah. That'd be nice.

JEREMY: You know who else I'd like to be?

DARRELL: Ronald McDonald?

JEREMY: No, man. The guy at the games, all the games—basketball, football, baseball—you name it. The guy that plays "The Star-Spangled Banner."

DARRELL: You serious? How come you wanna be that guy?

JEREMY: Because when he plays that song, all the people in the whole place stand up. All he does is play that one song, and all those thousands of people stand up. God, I think that'd be so great.

> *Set becomes black.*
>
> *The Botkin apartment. Nine-thirty the same night.* JEREMY *is sitting at the table near the kitchen, eating a sandwich and drinking a glass of milk.*

ROSALIE [*enters through door off living room. She is dressed in a faded bathrobe and is rubbing cream on her face*]: I thought you had dinner.

> [*She sits across from him at the table.*]

JEREMY [*not looking at her, taking a bite of the sandwich*]: He had to—

ROSALIE [*interrupting him*]: Don't talk with your mouth full, Jeremy.

JEREMY [*slowly chews sandwich. Takes a gulp of milk. Wipes his arm across his mouth*]: We didn't have dinner. He had to leave. [*Continues to finish eating sandwich.*]

ROSALIE [*angrily*]: Typical. [*She leans back and folds her arms* *across her chest and glares at him. Demandingly*] Did you get the check? [JEREMY *picks up empty plate and glass and goes to kitchen.* ROSALIE *stands up and calls after him.*] I gotta have that check, Jeremy!

JEREMY [*returns from kitchen, opens wallet, and takes out five-dollar bill and hands it to* ROSALIE]: He gave me this.

ROSALIE [*grabs money, holds out bill, and looks at it disgustedly*]: That's all you came back with? [*Stares at bill, then stuffs it in her bathrobe pocket and crosses room to door.* JEREMY *stands, holding back of chair, looking helpless. She calls over her shoulder, before exit to bedroom.*] You're as worthless as he is!

> *Lights dim.* JEREMY *sits at table. One elbow is on the table and he props his forehead against his hand. He sits like this for a minute, then gets up and goes to the living room and grabs his Walkman from the coffee table. He puts on the earphones, fiddles with the dial, and returns to the kitchen. He sits again, leaning forward, elbows on the table, with his chin propped in his hands. After a few minutes he takes off the earphones and goes to the kitchen. He disappears for a minute, then returns holding phone, pulling cord, and leaning against the kitchen wall. Set darkens. A spot is on* JEREMY. *At the end of the stage another spot is on* DARRELL, *sitting in a chair, holding a phone.*

JEREMY: Darrell?

DARRELL: Hi, man. How's it goin'?

JEREMY [*pausing a moment, then, defeatedly*]: It's air balls—my life's just air balls. [*A pause. Hopelessly*] Nothing I do goes in.

DARRELL [*not really understanding*]: Hmmm.

JEREMY [*flatly*]: Mr. Sanduzi won't let me near Renee. My dad gives me five bucks and splits. I give it to my mom. She tells me I'm as worthless as he is. [*A pause. He pounds his thigh. Turns toward wall.*] Sometimes—some .... [*His voice catches.*]

DARRELL: Jeremy?

JEREMY [*holding phone, he leans his forehead against the wall, his back to the audience. His shoulders shake as he begins to cry quietly. After a few minutes, he takes a deep breath and wipes the back of his hand across his eyes. A long pause. Quietly*]: Sometimes I just wanna go to Lake Erie and walk off in the water. It'd be so cold, you'd just feel nothing. Just close your eyes and the water'd come all around and it'd be cold and you'd just feel nothing. [*A long silence*]

DARRELL: Hum, Jeremy.

JEREMY: What?

DARRELL: I said hum, man. Hum "The Star-Spangled Banner." [*A pause. Forcefully.*] Do it, man! Just do it!

> [*Hesitantly, Jeremy starts to hum the first few bars of "The Star-Spangled Banner," then stops, then starts again.*]

DARRELL [*stands up*]: I'm standing up, Jeremy. [JEREMY *stops humming, half smiles.*] Hum it again, Jeremy. I'm standing up. [JEREMY *hums as the light dims and the curtain drops slowly.*]

27

Life in Gangland

by Sandra Gardner

Membership in a group can help someone determine his or her identity. What happens, though, when it's dangerous to be part of a particular group? Reporter Sandra Gardner spoke with gang members for a book about street gangs in the United States. This is the first chapter of her book.

In southern California, a land of year-round blooming greenery, in pastel houses nestled in rolling hills, the young people grow twisted and die quickly. Here in these barrios [neighborhoods] of poverty, Chicano gangs, one of the most prevalent types in the Southwest, flourish. In this chapter, we will look at a Chicano gang, one type of traditional youth gang.

Life here has been affected by gangs for decades—generations, even. Fathers, uncles, and grandfathers have been "soldiers" for the barrio gang. There is even a name for the old-timers: veteranos, the 30-, 40-, and 50-year-old members of the gang.

The younger ones are taught by the older members before taking their place as soldiers on this senseless battlefield. They, in time, will teach still younger ones.

This is all they know. This is what they have learned. This is what their parents' lives were and what their children's lives will probably be.

"That's the way it is," says 16-year-old Marcos. He looks like any teenager you would see anywhere—except for his eyes. They are constantly darting, scouring the area for danger from enemies, rival gang members who don't even know their victims' real names but only the name of a neighborhood they have sworn to hate.

Marcos is a member of Compton Barrios Largo 36. Compton is a tough Chicano and black ghetto in the Los Angeles area. Thirty-six stands for the 3600 block of the street.

The block is southern California-style poor. Junked cars litter the tight spaces between the squat pink and green broken-down dwellings and the tall, flourishing palms.

The Largo gang "watches out" for this neighborhood, say the members of its crew, who range in age from early puberty to nearly 30 years old. There are about 65 active members, not counting the "homeboys"—fellow gang members—in jail.

"When they come out, they'll be back with us," said Jaime, 23. Saying he works in a tire shop, he points to a pile of auto debris. All he is doing, he claims, is "just taking care of myself and my home-boys."

Nineteen-year-old Edgar says, "I've been shot, just because they see you in their neighborhood and they just start shooting." Five years ago he was shot in the right leg. "I was in the wrong neighborhood at the wrong time." He shrugs. "I went to the hospital. They took out the bullet and sewed me up. That's it. No big deal."

Marcos has dark hair and eyes and wears a white T-shirt and black pants, the uniform of a barrio gang. He has added an L.A. Raiders cap. His associates sometimes add a personal touch to the outfit: a gold cross, a button, a pin. Some have "Largo" printed on their caps. Others sew the name on their jackets. The basic uniform—T-shirt and black or khaki pants worn low at the waist—stays the same.

The name Largo can be seen scrawled on caps, jackets, and walls. That name and the gang it stands for have influenced the lives of these young people since early childhood. The gang so pervades life here that even attending school can be life-threatening.

Seventeen-year-old Alex, who sports the beginnings of a beard, says, "When I went to school yesterday, I got jumped [beaten up] by another gang. They went up to me and said, 'Tell me where you're from.'"

Asking and answering the question about one's home address is a direct invitation to violence. Because gangs are turf-oriented, the very fact of living in a particular location is enough reason to be attacked, shot at, or run over by a car. It doesn't matter to the enemies of a gang like Largo if the suspect is guilty of having done violence to the other crew, or if the young person unfortunate enough to live in Largo territory is even a member of the gang. Living there is reason enough—or not living there, as Marcos and his pals' vigilant scouring of their barrio for intruders testifies.

Alex's response in the school yard was reason enough for him to get beaten up. Badly. "When I said, 'Largo 36,' the other guy sent a man from their gang, and he started hitting me. I started hitting back, but then there were four of them. Then it was four of us from Largo against four Paragons and ten from Compton Trece and some from 155th Street."

In most gangs, the idea is to hype the macho. Being the toughest gang, the ones who can take it even when they're outnumbered, inflates their image of themselves and furthers their reputation.

"That's the only way they come to Largo, when there's more of them than us," Alex maintains, "but we can hang with [hold our own with] all of them gangs."

Says Marcos, "We'll hang in school, maybe for a couple of years. But some of the other gangs know we're up there and might go looking for us. So after a while maybe we don't go to school anymore."

One of the neighboring middle schools was the scene of sprayed bullets recently. A member of one gang, seeking revenge on another gang, went to the school yard and opened fire through the playground fence. Fortunately no one died—that day.

In June, 1990, the guests at a high-school graduation party in nearby Norwalk weren't so lucky.

Like millions of teenagers all over the country, the graduating seniors were celebrating in a friend's backyard. But in these parts, backyards are borders of rival gang territory. In this case the wall separating two houses marked the boundary between two violent barrio gangs: Chivas and Norwalk. They had been at each other for several years, resulting in over 30 shootings in the one square mile of sidewalk and buildings. The bloodshed at the party occurred over what should have been a relaxing Memorial Day weekend.

But for those gang members who did go to school and their families and friends, the June graduation party was designated by rivals as payback time.

From the dimly lit outdoors into the middle of the music, dancing, eating, and drinking, a voice shouted the name of the rivals. Within minutes unseen hands pulled the triggers of pistols and semiautomatics. The celebrants ran through the dark, screaming and falling.

The toll: one dead, nine critically wounded. Shooters and victims were 16, 17, 18 years old.

"It's the fourth gang-related murder in Norwalk in six months," said one law-enforcement officer.

In that same square mile, last year's casualty list included a 16-year-old boy. He is paralyzed from the waist down now, blinded in one eye, and unable to speak. He was run over by gang members driving a truck. His crime? Riding his bike in his neighborhood. A 17-year-old neighbor can't walk without crutches now. While he was walking home, a car drove by, and someone yelled out the name of a rival gang and then shot him. Three of his friends were shot last year in much the same circumstances.

About half the victims of gang violence are simply in the wrong place at the wrong time. They are innocent bystanders, like more than two dozen children and adults recently shot at in the streets of New York City. But other victims are a part of the payback cycle themselves. Often it is hard to tell who's who, since barrio and gang are intertwined for so many young people.

"We're a neighborhood," says Jaime. "We're all homies. We take care of our neighborhood."

Marcos considers himself lucky. "Every time they shoot at me, I'm down on the ground outside a car. They'll come by and shoot at me but hardly ever hit me. They shoot at us walking in the street. They come over here, shoot—and leave. They come to see where we'll be kicking back [hanging out]. I'll be catching them in my neighborhood and say, 'What are you doing in my neighborhood?' They start shooting at us and we'll make them get out. Then we'll get them back, throw our sign 'Largo' at them and get them back."

It's always the other guy who starts the violence, in the recounting of an incident. But it has been going on for so long that no one can remember who fired the first round. Actually, in the past, the war was fought with fists and bats and chains, not the heavy artillery of today. And not the cars. Today's gang warfare is conducted from a "low rider" car with its suspension lowered nearly to the ground.

Prison isn't even the end of it, unless a rival gang member pays someone back in jail.

"We've got homies in prison—county, state," says Jaime. "They go away, but they'll be out one of these days. They'll come out and do the same thing."

Like Marcos, who just came out, he says, for stealing cars. Marriage and children don't end it, either.

"Some are older already, they got kids," says Edgar. "But they just come kick back with us. In case something happens, they're right there to help us out."

Male or female doesn't matter here. Only the neighborhood.

"We look out for the girls," says Alex. "And the girls look out for us. In case something happens to us, the girls will go. And in case something happens to them, we'll be there for them."

Though there are few girls' gangs, girls will join the boys' groups. Or, if they live in a gang neighborhood or have a boyfriend in a gang, they will, at times, serve alongside the boys as soldiers and, consequently, as victims in this war zone.

In the back of a car the Largo crew is working on, a bunch of homegirls talk rapidly in English spiced with Spanish street language. They're 15, 16, 17, very pretty, heavily made up, and full of life. But, like their male counterparts, they're jaded and they take an I-don't-care attitude toward the future.

Sixteen-year-old Ana has long, dark hair and wears a white bow tucked behind her ear. "We're all homegirls," she says. "We don't have a leader."

"Equal opportunity," says 17-year-old Grace, who sports a thick mop of curly hair.

How many are in their crew?

"It's a lot," says 17-year-old Sandra. "About 50 of us."

What do they do?

They answer as one: "Kick back."

The peer pressure is so strong here that there is a uniform

language as well as a dress code and attitude. There is no other identity, nothing else to depend on, except one another.

"You get used to the shooting," says Ana. "Everybody's been shot at."

"The neighborhood we live in, what can you expect?" says Grace. "Everyday where we live, it's like a daily routine."

"Of course you're scared." Ana shrugs. "But you get used to it."

Why are they shot at?

"Because," says 17-year-old Else, "they think we're from another group."

Who is doing the shooting?

"Hispanics, blacks, it don't matter," says Grace.

"They're color-blind down there, man," Ana says emphatically. "They'll shoot at you. They won't care. If you're down in one neighborhood, that means you're going to be down to be shot."

Anybody dead?

"A lot," says Elsa. "Don't remind me. One of my friends got shot."

At a time when they should be looking toward a future, they know with a solid certainty that they have none. Homeboys, homegirls— many won't live into adulthood. Or they will be widowed, paralyzed, or blinded from gunfire.

"We know we're risking ourselves every time we go out of our house," says Ana.

"It's not because you want to do something bad," says Grace. "All you want to do is kick back."

"You go," says 17-year-old Maria. "You kick back, and maybe you get shot at. That's it."

"Otherwise," Ana explains, "you have to just stay inside your house."

Even that isn't any guarantee. Rival gang fights spill over into living rooms and bedrooms. In some neighborhoods people sleep on the floor, driven by the fear of bullets exploding through their windows.

If there is any hope of escape from the dead-end streets, it might be in the terrible knowledge that Marcos has accumulated during the first 16 years of his life.

"We know we're going to die one of these days. But we die in our neighborhood. I know what's happening to me," he says, his eyes quiet for a moment. "I tell my younger brother—he's 13—what's going up with the gang, so he don't join. I tell him, so it won't happen to him."

My Inner Shrimp

by Garry Trudeau

No matter how much you grow, once you've been looked down on, you'll never walk tall. Garry Trudeau, creator of Doonesbury, *remembers his sad, short past.*

For the rest of my days, I shall be a recovering short person. Even from my lofty perch of something over six feet (as if I don't know within a micron), I have the soul of a shrimp. I feel the pain of the diminutive, irrespective of whether they feel it themselves, because my visit to the planet of the teenage midgets was harrowing, humiliating, and extended. I even perceive my last-minute escape to have been flukish, somehow unearned—as if the Commissioner of Growth Spurts had been an old classmate of my father.

My most recent reminder of all this came the afternoon I went hunting for a new office. I had noticed a building under construction in my neighborhood—a brick warren of duplexes, with wide, westerly-facing windows, promising ideal light for a working studio. When I was ushered into the model unit, my pulse quickened: the soaring, 22-foot living room walls were gloriously aglow with the remains of the day. I bonded immediately.

Almost as an afterthought, I ascended the staircase to inspect the loft, ducking as I entered the bedroom. To my great surprise, I stayed ducked: the room was a little more than six feet in height. While my head technically cleared the ceiling, the effect was excruciatingly oppressive. This certainly wasn't a space I wanted to spend any time in, much less take out a mortgage on.

Puzzled, I wandered down to the sales office and asked if there were any other units to look at. No, replied a resolutely unpleasant receptionist, it was the last one. Besides, they were all exactly alike.

"Are you aware of how low the bedroom ceilings are?" I asked.

She shot me an evil look. "Of course we are," she snapped. "There were some problems with the building codes. The architect knows all about the ceilings.

"He's not an idiot, you know," she added, perfectly anticipating my next question.

She abruptly turned away, but it was too late. She'd just confirmed that a major New York developer, working with a fully licensed architect, had knowingly created an entire 12-story apartment building virtually uninhabitable by anyone of even average height. It was an exclusive high-rise for shorties.

Once I knew that, of course, I couldn't stay away. For days thereafter, as I walked to work, some perverse, unreasoning force would draw me back to the building. But it wasn't just the absurdity, the stone silliness of its design that had me in its grip; it was something far more compelling. Like some haunted veteran come again to an ancient battlefield, I was revisiting my perilous past.

When I was 14, I was the third-smallest in a high-school class of 100 boys, routinely mistaken for a sixth grader. My first week of school, I was drafted into a contingent of students ignominiously dubbed the "Midgets," so grouped by taller boys presumably so they could taunt us with more perfect efficiency. Inexplicably, some of my fellow Midgets refused to be diminished by the experience, but I retreated into self-pity. I sent away for a book on how to grow tall, and committed to memory its tips on overcoming one's genetic destiny— or at least making the most of a regrettable situation. The book cited historical figures who had gone the latter route—Alexander the

Great, Caesar, Napoleon (the mind involuntarily added Hitler). Strategies for stretching the limbs were suggested—hanging from door frames, sleeping on your back, doing assorted floor exercises— all of which I incorporated into my daily routine (get up, brush teeth, hang from door frame). I also learned the importance of meeting girls early in the day, when, the book assured me, my rested spine rendered me perceptibly taller.

For six years, my condition persisted; I grew, but at nowhere near the rate of my peers. I perceived other problems as ancillary, and loaded up the stature issue with freight shipped in daily from every corner of my life. Lack of athletic success, the absence of a social life, the inevitable run-ins with bullies—all could be attributed to the missing inches. The night I found myself sobbing in my father's arms was the low point; we both knew it was one problem he couldn't fix.

Of course what we couldn't have known was that he and my mother already had. They had given me a delayed developmental timetable. In my 17th year, I miraculously shot up six inches, just in time for graduation and a fresh start. I was, in the space of a few months, reborn—and I made the most of it. Which is to say that thereafter, all of life's disappointments, reversals, and calamities still arrived on schedule—but blissfully free of subtext.

Once you stop being the butt, of course, any problem recedes, if only to give way to a new one. And yet the impact of being literally looked down on, of being made to feel small, is forever. It teaches you how to stretch, how to survive the scorn of others for things that are beyond your control. Not growing forces you to grow up fast.

Sometimes I think I'd like to return to a high-school reunion to surprise my classmates. Not that they didn't know me when I finally started catching up. They did, but I doubt they'd remember. Adolescent hierarchies have a way of enduring; I'm sure I am still recalled as the Midget I myself have never really left behind.

Of course, if I'm going to show up, it'll have to be soon. I'm starting to shrink.

The Death of Me

by Gordon Lish

The narrator of this story remembers being ten years old on a day when he seemed to be amazing. Why, then, did he feel so strange?

I wanted to be amazing. I wanted to be so amazing. I had already been amazing up to a certain point. But I was tired of being at that point. I wanted to go past that point. I wanted to be more amazing than I had been up to that point. I wanted to do something which went beyond that point and which went beyond every other point and which people would look at and say that this was something which went beyond all other points and which no other boy would ever be able to go beyond, that I was the only boy who could, that I was the only one.

I was going to a day camp which was called the Peninsula Athletes Day Camp and which at the end of the summer had an all-campers, all-parents, all-sports field day which was made up of five different field events and all of the campers had to take part in all five of all of the different field events, and I was the winner in all five of the five different field events, I was the winner in every single field event, I came in first place in every one of the five different field events—so that the head of the camp and the camp counselors and the other campers and the other mothers and the other fathers and my mother and my father all saw that I was the best camper in the Peninsula Athletes Day Camp, the best in the short run and the best in the long run and the best in the high jump and the best in the broad jump and the best in the event which the Peninsula Athletes Day Camp called the ball-throw, which was where you had to go up to a chalk line and then put your toe on the chalk line and not go over the chalk line and then throw the ball as far as you could throw.

I did.

I won.

It was 1944 and I was ten years old and I was better than all of the other boys at that camp and probably all of the boys everywhere else.

I felt more wonderful than I had ever felt. I felt so thrilled with myself. I felt like God was whispering things to me inside of my head. I felt like God was asking me to have a special secret with him or to have a secret arrangement with him and that I had to keep listening to his secret recommendations to me inside of my head. I felt like God was telling me to realize that he had made me the most unusual member of the human race and that he was going to need me to be ready for him to go to work for him at any minute for him on whatever thing he said.

They gave me a piece of stiff cloth which was in the shape of a shield and which was in the camp colors and which had five blue stars on it. They said that I was the only boy ever to get a shield with as many as that many stars on it. They said that it was unheard-of for any boy ever to get as many as that many stars on it. But I could already feel that I was forgetting what it felt like to do something which would get you a shield with as many as that many stars on it. I could feel myself forgetting and I could feel everybody else forgetting, even my mother and father and God forgetting. It was just a little while afterwards, but I could tell that everybody was already forgetting everything about it—the head of the camp and the camp counselors and the other campers and the other mothers and the other fathers and my mother and my father and even that I myself was, even though I was trying with all of my might to be the one person who never would.

I felt like God was ashamed of me. I felt like God was sorry that I was the one which he had picked out and that he was getting ready to make a new choice and to choose another boy instead of me and that I had to hurry up before God did it, that I had to be quick about showing God that I could be just as amazing again as I used to be and that I could do something better or at least do something else.

It was August.

I was feeling the strangest feeling that I have ever felt. I was standing there with my parents and with all of the people who had come there for the field day and I was feeling the strangest feeling which I have ever felt.

I felt like lying down on the field. I felt like killing all of the people. I felt like going to sleep and staying asleep until someone came and told me that my parents were dead and that I was all grown up now and that there was a new God in heaven and that he liked me better even than the old God had.

My parents kept asking me where did I want to go now and what did I want to do. My parents kept trying to get me to tell them where I thought we should all go now and what was the next thing for us as a family to do. My parents wanted for me to be the one to make up my mind if we should all go someplace special now and what was the best thing for the family, as a family, to do. But I did not know what they meant—do, do, do?

My father took the shield away from me and held it in his hands and kept turning it over and over in his hands and kept looking at the shield and feeling the shield and saying that it was made of buckram and felt. My father kept saying did we know that it was just something which they had put together out of buckram and felt. My father kept saying that the shield was of a very nice quality of buckram and was of a very nice quality of felt but that we should make every effort not to get it wet now because it would run all over itself.

I did not know what to do.

I could tell that my parents did not know what to do.

We just stood around and people were going away to all of the vehicles that were going to take them to places and I could tell that we did not know if it was time for us to go.

The head of the camp came over and said that he wanted to shake my hand again and shake the hands of the people who were responsible for giving the Peninsula Athletes Day Camp such an outstanding young individual and such a talented young athlete as my mother and father had.

He shook my hand again.

It made me feel dizzy and nearly asleep.

I saw my mother and my father get their hands ready. I saw my father get the shield out of the hand that he thought he was going to need for him to have his hand ready to shake the hand of the head of the camp. I saw my mother take her purse and do the same thing. But the head of the camp just kept shaking my hand, and my mother and my father just kept saying thank you to him, and then the head of the camp let go of my hand and took my father's elbow with one hand and then touched my father on the shoulder with the other hand and then said that we were certainly the very finest of people, and then he went—he did this, he did this!—then he went away.

Warning

by Jenny Joseph

When I am an old woman I shall wear purple
With a red hat which doesn't go, and doesn't suit me,
And I shall spend my pension on brandy and summer gloves
And satin sandals, and say we've no money for butter.
I shall sit down on the pavement when I'm tired
And gobble up samples in shops and press alarm bells
And run my stick along the public railings
And make up for the sobriety of my youth.
I shall go out in my slippers in the rain
And pick the flowers in other people's gardens
And learn to spit.

You can wear terrible shirts and grow more fat
And eat three pounds of sausage at a go
Or only bread and pickle for a week
And hoard pens and pencils and beermats and things in boxes.

But now we must have clothes that keep us dry
And pay the rent and not swear in the street
And set a good example for the children.
We must have friends to dinner and read the papers.

But maybe I ought to practice a little now?
So people who know me are not too shocked and surprised
When suddenly I am old and start to wear purple.

Ode to Weight Lifting

by Gary Soto

Tony eats apples
On Saturday morning,
Two for each arm,
And one for the backs
Of his calves.
He's twelve
And a weight lifter in his
  garage.
He bites into an apple,
And, chewing,
He curls weights—
One, two, three . . .
His face reddens,
And a blue vein
Deepens on his neck—
Four, five, six . . .
Sweat inches down
His cheek. A curl of
Hair falls in his face—
Seven, eight, nine . . .
He grunts and strains—
Ten, eleven, twelve!

Tony curls his age,
And he would curl his weight
Of 83 pounds, but he
Would pull a muscle
In his arm.

Tony pulls off his T-shirt.
He flexes his biceps,
And apples show up in his
  arms.
"Pretty good," he says,
His fists clenched.
He takes another
Bite of apple,
And out of happiness
Bites the apples
In his biceps, tenderly
Of course. The teeth
Marks are pink,
His arms brown,
And his roar red as a lion's
With a paw swiping at air.

An Hour with Abuelo

by Judith Ortiz Cofer

Arturo is reluctant to visit his grandfather in a nursing home. He doesn't realize how much he can learn about his abuelo *in just one hour.*

"Just one hour, *una hora,* is all I'm asking of you, son." My grandfather is in a nursing home in Brooklyn, and my mother wants me to spend some time with him, since the doctors say that he doesn't have too long to go now. *I* don't have much time left of my summer vacation, and there's a stack of books next to my bed I've got to read if I'm going to get into the AP English class I want. I'm going stupid in some of my classes, and Mr. Williams, the principal at Central, said that if I passed some reading tests, he'd let me move up.

Besides, I hate the place, the old people's home, especially the way it smells like industrial-strength ammonia and other stuff I won't mention, since it turns my stomach. And really the abuelo always has a lot of relatives visiting him, so I've gotten out of going out there except at Christmas, when a whole vanload of grandchildren are herded over there to give him gifts and a hug. We all make it quick and spend the rest of the time in the recreation area, where they play checkers and stuff with some of the old people's games, and I catch up on back issues of *Modern Maturity*. I'm not picky, I'll read almost anything.

Anyway, after my mother nags me for about a week, I let her drive me to Golden Years. She drops me off in front. She wants me to go in alone and have a "good time" talking to Abuelo. I tell her to be back in one hour or I'll take the bus back to Paterson. She squeezes my hand and says, *"Gracias, hijo,"* in a choked-up voice like I'm doing her a big favor.

I get depressed the minute I walk into the place. They line up the old people in wheelchairs in the hallway as if they were about to be raced to the finish line by orderlies who don't even look at them when they push them here and there. I walk fast to room 10, Abuelo's "suite." He is sitting up in his bed writing with a pencil in one of those old-fashioned black hardback notebooks. It has the outline of the island of Puerto Rico on it. I slide into the hard vinyl chair by his bed. He sort of smiles and the lines on his face get deeper, but he doesn't say anything. Since I'm supposed to talk to him, I say, "What are you doing, Abuelo, writing the story of your life?"

It's supposed to be a joke, but he answers, *"Sí,* how did you know, Arturo?"

His name is Arturo too. I was named after him. I don't really know my grandfather. His children, including my mother, came to New York and New Jersey (where I was born) and he stayed on the Island until my grandmother died. Then he got sick, and since nobody could leave their jobs to go take care of him, they brought him to this nursing home in Brooklyn. I see him a couple of times a year, but he's always surrounded by his sons and daughters. My mother tells me that Don Arturo had once been a teacher back in Puerto Rico, but had lost his job after the war. Then he became a farmer. She's always saying in a sad voice, *"Ay, bendito!* What a waste of a fine mind." Then she usually shrugs her shoulders and says, *"Así es la vida."* That's the way life is. It sometimes makes me mad that the adults I know just accept whatever crap is thrown at them because "that's the way things are." Not for me. I go after what I want.

Anyway, Abuelo is looking at me like he was trying to see into my head, but he doesn't say anything. Since I like stories, I decide I may as well ask him if he'll read me what he wrote.

I look at my watch: I've already used up 20 minutes of the hour I promised my mother.

Abuelo starts talking in his slow way. He speaks what my mother calls book English. He taught himself from a dictionary, and his words sound stiff, like he's sounding them out in his head before he says them. With his children he speaks Spanish, and that funny book English with us grandchildren. I'm surprised that he's still so sharp, because his body is shrinking like a crumpled-up brown paper sack with some bones in it. But I can see from looking into his eyes that the light is still on in there.

"It is a short story, Arturo. The story of my life. It will not take very much time to read it."

"I have time, Abuelo." I'm a little embarrassed that he saw me looking at my watch.

"Yes, *hijo*. You have spoken the truth. *La verdad.* You have much time."

Abuelo reads: "'I loved words from the beginning of my life. In the *campo* where I was born one of seven sons, there were few books. My mother read them to us over and over: The Bible, the stories of Spanish conquistadors and of pirates that she had read as a child and brought with her from the city of Mayagüez; that was before she married my father, a coffee bean farmer; and she taught us words from the newspaper that a boy on a horse brought every week to her. She taught each of us how to write on a slate with chalks that she ordered by mail every year. We used those chalks until they were so small that you lost them between your fingers.

"'I always wanted to be a writer and a teacher. With my heart and my soul I knew that I wanted to be around books all of my life. And so against the wishes of my father, who wanted all his sons to help him on the land, she sent me to high school in Mayagüez. For four years I boarded with a couple she knew. I paid my rent in labor, and I ate vegetables I grew myself. I wore my clothes until they were thin as parchment. But I graduated at the top of my class! My whole family came to see me that day. My mother brought me a beautiful *guayabera,* a white shirt made of the finest cotton and embroidered by her own hands. I was a happy young man.

"'In those days you could teach in a country school with a high school diploma. So I went back to my mountain village and got a job teaching all grades in a little classroom built by the parents of my students.

"'I had books sent to me by the government. I felt like a rich man although the pay was very small. I had books. All the books I wanted! I taught my students how to read poetry and plays, and how to write them. We made up songs and put on shows for the parents. It was a beautiful time for me.

"'Then the war came, and the American President said that all Puerto Rican men would be drafted. I wrote to our governor and explained that I was the only teacher in the mountain village. I told him that the children would go back to the fields and grow up ignorant if I could not teach them their letters. I said that I thought I was a better teacher than a soldier. The governor did not answer my letter. I went into the U.S. Army.

"'I told my sergeant that I could be a teacher in the army. I could teach all the farm boys their letters so that they could read the instructions on the ammunition boxes and not blow themselves up. The sergeant said I was too smart for my own good, and gave me a job cleaning latrines. He said to me there is reading material for you there, scholar. Read the writing on the walls. I spent the war mopping floors and cleaning toilets.

"'When I came back to the Island, things had changed. You had to have a college degree to teach school, even the lower grades. My parents were sick, two of my brothers had been killed in the war, the others had stayed in Nueva York. I was the only one left to help the old people. I became a farmer. I married a good woman who gave me many good children. I taught them all how to read and write before they started school.'"

Abuelo then puts the notebook down on his lap and closes his eyes.

"*Así es la vida* is the title of my book," he says in a whisper, almost to himself. Maybe he's forgotten that I'm there.

For a long time he doesn't say anything else. I think that he's sleeping, but then I see that he's watching me through half-closed lids, maybe waiting for my opinion of his writing. I'm trying to think of something nice to say. I liked it and all, but not the title. And I think that he could've been a teacher if he had wanted to bad enough. Nobody is going to stop me from doing what I want with my life. I'm not going to let *la vida* get in my way. I want to discuss this with him, but the words are not coming into my head in Spanish just yet. I'm about to ask him why he didn't keep fighting to make his dream come true, when an old lady in hot-pink running shoes sort of appears at the door.

She is wearing a pink jogging outfit too. The world's oldest marathoner, I say to myself. She calls out to my grandfather in a flirty voice, "Yoo-hoo, Arturo, remember what day this is? It's poetry-reading day in the rec room! You promised us you'd read your new one today."

I see my abuelo perking up almost immediately. He points to his wheelchair, which is hanging like a huge metal bat in the open closet. He makes it obvious that he wants me to go get it. I put it together, and with Mrs. Pink Running Shoes's help, we get him in it. Then he says in a strong deep voice I hardly recognize, "Arturo, get that notebook from the table, please."

I hand him another map-of-the-Island notebook—this one is red. On it in big letters it says, *POEMAS DE ARTURO.*

I start to push him toward the rec room, but he shakes his finger at me.

"Arturo, look at your watch now. I believe your time is over." He gives me a wicked smile.

Then with her pushing the wheelchair—maybe a little too fast—they roll down the hall. He is already reading from his notebook, and she's making bird noises. I look at my watch and the hour *is* up, to the minute. I can't help but think that my abuelo has been timing *me.* It cracks me up. I walk slowly down the hall toward the exit sign. I want my mother to have to wait a little. I don't want her to think that I'm in a hurry or anything.

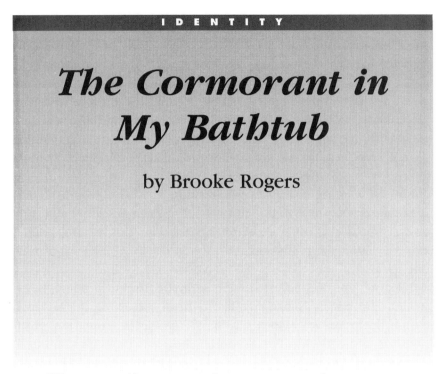

The Cormorant in My Bathtub

by Brooke Rogers

Who are we if no one needs us or wants us?

When I was about eight, I went to live with my grandparents at the beach. I had never seen the ocean before, and to this day the memory is vivid. We pulled into the driveway at dusk, and I could see behind the house an exciting expanse of untouched water. I shivered. Since my parents died, I had not felt any emotion; I had been only a breathing vegetable. But now I could feel the blood beginning to pump through my veins. I felt warm and tingly. The colors of the horizon and the dying sun were a shimmer of pinks and purples. The sun, arrayed in its most beautiful gown, was ready to die valiantly. I was sure even the Garden of Eden could not have been more beautiful.

From that moment on I was madly in love with the ocean. I lay in the sand for hours watching the cormorants circling over the lapping waves. How I envied those birds, their graceful black bodies circling and diving into the brilliant waters. They did not know fear or sadness; they knew only life, sun, and the ocean. They would plummet into the sea at tremendous speeds, and not once did they miss their prey. There were no failures. Each one always emerged with a silver minnow speared on its beak.

Every day from sunup to sundown I haunted the beach. I never tried to make new friends; I was always alone. I dreaded the first day of school. I was always dreaming that I would become a cormorant and fly away over the ocean, never to be seen again.

It was a Wednesday night when the tanker sank. The rain was falling in solid sheets, the wind blowing at nearly fifty knots! All the power lines were out; even the glow of the lighthouse was not strong enough to pierce the storm. The captain of the tanker lost his course and ran aground on Lookout Point. The side of the tanker split on the rocks, spilling hundreds of thousands of gallons of oil into the raging sea.

The next day the ocean was calm, but the waves that lapped against the beach were tainted. Riding on the waves were the black remains of the oil tanker's cargo. I watched in horror as helpless sea birds struggled to stay afloat, flapping their wings in frenzied splashes as they tried desperately to free themselves from the clinging oil. Tears streamed down my cheeks as I dashed into the ocean and gathered up as many birds as I could capture. I returned to the house and filled the bathtub with clean, fresh water. Then I pried open as many beaks as I could. I watched helplessly as the birds surrendered to the clinging grease that clogged their nostrils and held fast their beaks. My whole body shook with grief. I lifted their limp bodies and tenderly set them on a towel. Among the dead were three gulls, two sandpipers, and one brown pelican.

One bird remained in the tub, a black bird who would not give up. He lay quietly in the tub, but his eyes were alert, and he was wide awake. He was a cormorant. To take my mind off the others, I picked him up and began to rub his back with tissue and detergent. It took hours, but the bird seemed to sense that I was trying to help. He lay still and allowed me to wipe every last drop of oil off his glossy back. When I placed him back in the tub he drank deeply, enjoying the strange, sweet taste of fresh water for the first time.

When my grandma found me she did not scold me for making a

mess of her guest bathroom. She simply asked if I would like some help burying the dead birds. Without asking, I knew she would let the cormorant stay in her bathtub. The bird was clearly exhausted. He lay motionless with his head tucked under his wing. As we buried the six birds, I wondered what would happen to the seventh.

For a week my grandparents forbade me to visit the beach. I knew that the oil was still thick and that the white sand would never be quite as pure. We had numerous wildlife representatives visit our beach and collect water samples and gather up dead fish and birds. They would often stop and look in on my bird, but they never tried to take him away. I fed him sardines and tuna fish. He ate greedily and slowly became stronger. Sadly, I realized that my new friend would need to leave me.

A few kids in my neighborhood stopped by to see the bird. Grandma encouraged them to stay for tea, and I was surprised at how much fun we had. The more time I spent with the neighborhood kids, the more I looked forward to the opening of school. The water was regaining its purity and soon it would be safe to let the bird go. He would once again be searching the sea for a school of minnows instead of splashing about in our bathtub. Still, I did not like to think about losing him.

Two weeks after the storm, school started. I was excited by new classes and new friends. I was spending very little time on the beach. Instead, I had been playing baseball in the lot behind our house. I felt needed and wanted for the first time since my parents' death; the black bird in my bathtub needed me, and my friends wanted me to play third base and share adventures with them.

On the third day of school I returned home to find the bird gone. The door was shut tight, but the window was open and the curtain was blowing in the breeze. On the floor below the window a long black feather rested. I picked it up and stroked the smooth edge as I thought of all the bird had given me.

Song

by Adrienne Rich

You're wondering if I'm lonely:
OK then, yes, I'm lonely
as a plane rides lonely and level
on its radio beam, aiming
across the Rockies
for the blue-strung aisles
of an airfield on the ocean

You want to ask, am I lonely?
Well, of course, lonely
as a woman driving across country
day after day, leaving behind
mile after mile
little towns she might have stopped
and lived and died in, lonely

If I'm lonely
it must be the loneliness
of waking first, of breathing
dawn's first cold breath on the city
of being the one awake
in a house wrapped in sleep

If I'm lonely
it's with the rowboat ice-fast on the shore
in the last red light of the year
that knows what it is, that knows it's neither
ice nor mud nor winter light
but wood, with a gift for burning

The Nightmare

by Megan Whalen Turner

Acting tough can lead to dangerous consequences, as seventh-grader Kevin discovers. Then he finds himself changing in important ways. Will the nightmare ever end?

Summer vacation had long since trailed off into empty days and boredom. Twice that afternoon the boys had been chased away from the bus stop, where they liked to hang out, making boasts and idle plans. The manager of Orly's deli stepped out of his doorway ready to chase them away a third time; the bus stop benches were for people who used the buses, not for a bunch of near adolescents who had nothing to do with their time but make trouble.

With their hands in their pockets and their chins in the air, the boys prepared to move on, pretending to themselves that it was their decision, not somebody's pushing, that was making them go, when a bus pulled up and squeezed out a puddle of tired commuters.

It was Kevin's idea to follow the dowdy old woman. He gestured to his friends, and they fell in behind him. Walking tough with their hands still in their pockets and their shoulders rolled forward, they followed her up the sidewalk until she turned off on 54th Street. They turned the corner as well and pulled a little closer. The old woman glanced back. She wasn't really old, not much older than Kevin's mother. Her skin was smooth, but the hair that pushed out from under her knit hat was streaked with gray. Her dress was gray, as well as the coat she wore. She was dingy and drab and not very interesting. Kevin wasn't sure why he had chosen to follow her.

The woman turned left at Blackstone Avenue. When she looked back again, she could no longer pretend that coincidence kept her and the boys on a shared path. She put her head down and walked faster.

Kevin, stepping along in front of his friends, matched her speed, feeling proud of the anxiety a group of seventh graders could inspire. He and his friends had never done anything like this. Although they'd bullied the younger kids at school, they'd never before intimidated an adult. He thought it was a turning point. No doubt when school started in a few days, Kevin and his friends would be able to make even the high-school kids sit up and take notice. Absorbed in his daydreams of power, he didn't notice that the woman ahead of him had stopped until he almost ran into her. Startled, he stepped back and bumped the boy behind him.

"Well, what do you want from me?" the woman snapped with a ferocity that hadn't been there only a moment before.

Kevin felt the blood rushing to his face as his daydreams broke up. He felt foolish and was afraid to be laughed at by his friends. He swept his shattered dignity together and said in a cocky voice, "I want whatever you've got." Behind him, his friends stirred nervously. They had been teasing the old woman for fun, and Kevin was pushing things further than they were willing to go. Their hesitation drove him on.

"Come on, lady, what have you got?"

"This is what I've got and you can have it." She pulled her hand from her coat pocket and threw something at him. He cupped his hands in front of his chest and caught it there. Something that felt like a blob of Jell-O smacked into his palms, but when he looked, his hands were empty. He looked up again as the woman disappeared into a nearby apartment building. The lock on the door clicked shut behind her.

Kevin looked down at the sidewalk to see if he had dropped whatever it was. He saw nothing. He shrugged. "Come on, let's go up to Walgreen's. Get some candy and stuff."

That night, Kevin lay in bed listening to the television that was on in the living room. It was a murder mystery that his parents were watching. Listening to the dialogue, Kevin tried to visualize the story in his head. The lady had told everyone that she knew who the killer was, even though she didn't. She just guessed. But she thought that if she pretended she had evidence, the killer would come after her and then she would have proof to take to the police. Now she was alone in the house at night and the killer was getting closer. There were long periods of silence broken by little crackling noises and suspense music. Kevin figured the killer was lurking in the bushes outside the house. The lady in the house thought she was safe, but she wasn't. The killer was getting closer. He crept up the steps of the back porch. Kevin rolled over on his side. The killer started checking the windows to see which one was open. The killer stepped from the back porch to the ledge of Kevin's window, but it was safely locked. The killer rattled the frame just to be sure. Then he stepped back onto the porch. Kevin could hear him checking the lock on the kitchen door, turning the knob, and bumping the door back and forth. Kevin wanted to call for help, but he was alone. After a few minutes, the bumping stopped. Kevin relaxed.

Then he heard the creaking of steps in the stairwell. Somehow the killer had gotten through the front door of the apartment building. He was climbing the stairs to Kevin's apartment. Terrified, Kevin realized that his front door wasn't locked. He tried to jump out of bed and run down the hall to the door, but he couldn't move. Lying there in the dark, he heard the front door opening. He heard the footsteps in the hall, getting closer and closer. The killer was coming. He was bringing something horrible with him. He crept closer with each step until Kevin knew that the killer stood in the dark right outside his own bedroom door. Kevin couldn't see, but he knew the door was opening.

Kevin threw the covers off and jumped out of bed, ready to run, but there was no need. It was morning. The sun was coming in his window. The door to his bedroom was still closed. It had all been a nightmare. With his knees still shaking, Kevin got back in bed and huddled under the blankets.

The next night, giant snakes slid out of the ground all around the apartment building. They slithered through the dark, up the fire escapes, and across the back porch. They curled on the window ledges and pressed their cold bodies against the glass. Each one carried a mirror in its mouth that clicked and scratched against the window.

In the morning Kevin couldn't convince himself that the snakes weren't still there. He wouldn't leave the apartment until his sister had been outside and down the stairs without being eaten. By the time he found his friends at the basketball court, they had already chosen teams, and there was no room for Kevin to play.

After the third nightmare, Kevin was desperately happy to see the morning. He set off to the schoolyard, tired but cocksure, confident that the power he had wielded as a sixth grader in an elementary school would be waiting for him as a seventh grader in junior high. His confidence disappeared with his lunch money when kids from the high-school side of the building shook him down in the schoolyard.

Kevin had never been in a school where students changed classes with each subject. He didn't share a homeroom with his friends; he had no one to remind him that he was cool and tough and didn't need to be intimidated by a complicated schedule and unfamiliar teachers. He had to bully a couple of kids out of their small change to make himself feel better and get enough money for lunch.

Lunch should have been a pleasure. Kevin had never known a school cafeteria to sell ice-cream sandwiches. They were all he had money for, but they were all he wanted. He never saw the foot that snaked out and tripped him as he made his way to the junior-high side of the lunchroom. His lunch tray flew into the air as he stumbled to his knees. The whole lunchroom laughed. Somebody stepped on his sandwich.

In the afternoon he got lost and ended up in the high-school side of the school, where he was chased by the same group that had taken his lunch money in the schoolyard.

"Hey, Kevin," they called down the hallway, "we heard you're really tough."

"We heard you were the big man of the sixth grade."

"Big deal, Kevin."

They tipped his books out of his arms and left him with a scatter of papers to collect.

"We'll see you tomorrow, Kev. Don't forget your lunch money."

By the end of the day, Kevin had forgotten there was a reason to dread going to bed.

"Nothing," he said to himself as he settled between the sheets, "could be worse than today."

The giant snakes came back. This time they crawled up to the front door and slid beneath it. They came under the back door and through the bathroom drains. They slid down the hall to Kevin's door and bumped against the doorknob. Terrorized, Kevin buried his head under the covers. The snakes slid under his bed and came up along the walls. Kevin could feel them hunting through the rumpled blankets. When they found Kevin, they pushed their mirrors against his skin, cold and sharp and insistent. Kevin moaned. He kept his face hidden in the pillow until one very insistent poke forced him to turn over. He looked into one of the mirrors and saw a reflection of his day.

Over and over he watched himself handing over his money to the older boys. He writhed with misery and embarrassment as his ice-cream sandwich flew through the air, and again and again he watched the sneaker stamp down on it. He heard the whole lunchroom laughing in muffled roars like the noise of an underground train.

"Big man of the sixth grade, Kevin?" He was surrounded by high-school students, and he saw himself with their contempt and disgust. He relived every horrible scene of the day, and there was no relief. He saw himself bullying smaller kids and felt no surge of arrogance and power. Instead, he watched from their eyes, and he looked hateful and insecure. He didn't look tough. When he was trying hardest to look tough, he only looked ridiculous.

Mesmerized by the mirror, Kevin watched his whole day pass over and over until he had seen it from the viewpoint of every person he'd encountered and felt every person's opinion.

In the morning, he was exhausted. He dragged himself out of bed and made his way into the kitchen on shaking legs.

"Mom, I don't feel well. I don't want to go to school today."

His mother laughed. "Only one day and already school makes you sick? Go get your clothes on. There's nothing the matter with you that breakfast won't cure."

The days passed. The nights passed, too, but more slowly. No matter what he did, Kevin spent each night reviewing his actions with loathing. Every night the snakes came and prodded him with their mirrors until he dragged his face out of the pillow. In miserable and unavoidable detail, he watched himself through other people's eyes. Inevitably, anyone who noticed him did so with contempt or malicious amusement or loathing. The mildest emotion he ever registered was distaste from his science teacher No one was ever impressed by him; no one ever admired him. No one thought him good-looking or fashionably dressed.

Most unfair of all, he never once saw himself through the eyes of his friends. He would have protested this, he would have protested everything, but who was there to protest to? Instead, he tried to sound out his friends. He asked them about their dreams but lied about his own. Some of the other kids had had nightmares, but they didn't sound anything like his. Of course, how was he to know? If he was lying, maybe they were, too. He began asking trick questions, hoping to catch them in a lie, but this earned him a few strange looks, and he and his friends drifted further apart. They shared no classes, not even lunch, and somehow it was easy to avoid meeting them after school. Kevin found that if he went straight home and sat in his room, those hours at least would not show up in the mirrors at night.

Why, though, did everyone hate him so much? Why did no one ever think anything good about him? Couldn't he at least dream about what his friends thought, just once?

The apartment was locked the next day when he got home. His mother wouldn't be back for hours, so Kevin left his books by the door and went to look for the gang. They were surprised to see him, but they made room for him at the top of the fence next to the play lot. They spent the afternoon together. They stole a basketball from one of the littler kids and shot baskets for a while. Then they wandered down to the vacant lot by the train tracks and smoked cigarettes that Jerry had taken from his father. The rest of the gang wanted to go to Walgreen's to see if they could lift some candy, but

Kevin backed out. He had an idea already that his dreams would be bad. He could guess what the people in Walgreen's would think of him. He went home. He did his homework and ate dinner and went to bed.

That night, watching himself in the mirror, he saw himself through his friends' eyes. None of his friends liked him much. Since the first day of school, when they had watched him fork over his lunch money, they'd been embarrassed to have him around. Kevin wasn't cool. He was a nobody. Every day the high-school kids asked him for money, and every day Kevin handed it over just like all the other nobodies in the school.

In the morning, Kevin put his clothes on and, desperately miserable, headed to school. The first bell hadn't rung yet, and the yard was full of people talking about their boyfriends or girlfriends or future or ex-boyfriends or girlfriends. Everybody was making plans for the weekend. Kevin couldn't face his friends after the previous night's revelations. He turned left and walked around the school to the front entrance, one that was almost never used. It was deep in a recess formed by the gymnasium wall on one side and three stories of classrooms on the other. The sunlight passed right by without stopping. The wind swirled a couple of pieces of paper and a pop can in a corner against the steps while Kevin sat on the cold concrete steps and thought about how a perfectly normal life can turn into a disaster and all it takes is two weeks in the seventh grade

The bell rang. Kevin went inside. He dumped his books in his locker and moused his way through another day. He'd never done homework in the sixth grade, but he did it now. There was nothing else to occupy his time as he sat alone in his room every afternoon. And he found that he liked it. He liked the orderliness of mathematics once he understood the rules, and he got almost the same kick out of solving problems that he used to get stealing candy from Walgreen's. He wished his life were as easy to work as a math problem.

By using the school's front entrance, Kevin had avoided the high-school boys who usually relieved him of his lunch money. Having enough money for a regular lunch should have been a bright spot in his day. Unfortunately, he met one of the older boys as he was leaving the lunchroom. The older boy looked down at Kevin's substantial lunch and shook his head back and forth. Kevin scuttled away, realizing that he should have settled for an ice-cream bar; the hamburger stuck in his throat.

That night, when the snakes held up their mirrors, Kevin saw himself slinking down a school hallway, using his notebook as a shield. He was concentrating so hard on anonymity that it was only a particularly conscientious teacher who would have noticed him. Kevin felt the teacher's ripple of curiosity and distaste for the cringing figure. Then the dream moved on.

In the morning, Kevin thought there had been something familiar about that scurrying person in the dream. Of course it had to be familiar; he was watching himself. But there was something beyond that. When he got to school, he slipped around the building, looking for other open entrances. He had cheated the older boys of his lunch money the day before. They would be looking for him that morning. He sat on the steps on the far side of the gymnasium and thought about his problems until the bell rang.

For the next week, Kevin entered the school by various doors. He went through the music-room door. He waited once for the late bell to ring and snuck into the building through the auto shop. The older boys glared at him in the lunchroom, but Kevin was safe while in the building, and the junior high let out half an hour earlier than the high school. One of the gym doors didn't close properly, so Kevin slipped in that way twice. After school, he headed straight home without stopping to hassle any of the smaller kids. Seeing himself through those kids' eyes every night had taken the fun out of the bullying. Kevin's goal was to get through the day with no one noticing him at all.

While sitting alone in his room for hours, Kevin thought about his nightmares. The crouching mousy figure in his dreams rang a distant bell. Kevin racked his brains trying to understand. Finally, the next day, as he waited on the gymnasium steps, the bell rang right inside his head. The sloping walk that he saw in the dreams was the same as the walk of the Jell-O lady, the one he and his friends had been hassling just before school started. The rest of the day passed in a blur. Kevin didn't care what his dreams would be like that night. For the first time he thought he knew where they came from, and he hoped to get rid of them.

After school, he went straight to the bus stop at 55th and Hyde

Park Boulevard. He checked the passengers getting off every bus. He spent all day Saturday at the bus stop as well. He sat on the bench until the manager at Orly's chased him away. After that, he walked up and down the street, hurrying back to the bench whenever a bus arrived. She wasn't there. By Sunday, he was beginning to despair. What if that had been the only day she had ridden the bus? What if she had bought a car? What if, after ruining his life forever, she'd decided to move to Ohio or someplace like that? He walked up Blackstone Avenue trying to find her apartment building, but couldn't pick it out. Maybe he would never find her and he'd be stuck forever slinking down hallways like some sort of deformed rabbit.

He was late for dinner and should have started home, but he kept telling himself he would wait for just one more bus. Finally, he thought he saw her. Maybe. But she was wearing different clothes, a red coat and an orange dress, and she walked differently, swinging her arms and bobbing her chin, humming to herself as she walked. Kevin had seen her the day before but had not recognized her. He still wasn't sure if this was the woman he wanted or not. He followed her down the street. She turned at a familiar corner and headed for a familiar building.

"Wait," Kevin shouted as she put her key in the door.

She turned and recognized Kevin immediately. She laughed in his face.

"No backsies," she said. The door closed and locked behind her.

"Wait, wait!" Kevin threw himself against the door and rattled the lock. Through the dirty glass in the door he saw the woman disappear up the steps inside without looking back. After a moment, he sat down on the steps and hugged his knees. Eventually, he had to go home for dinner, but the next morning, when the woman came out to go to work, he was waiting on the step.

"What, are you still here?" she asked.

"What did you mean, 'no backsies'?" he asked.

"Just what I said. You can't give it back to me. You have to give it to someone else who asks for it."

"But what is it?"

"What do you think? It's a nightmare." She walked down the street.

Kevin met her when she got off the bus that afternoon. "Why did you give it to me?" he asked.

"Because you asked for it. Hassling an old woman and telling her you want whatever she's got. People who ask for it get what's coming to them."

"Then where did you get it?"

She stopped at the corner. She looked down at him and nodded her head as she admitted, "I asked for it."

"How long?"

"How long did I have it? Six years," she said softly.

Kevin rocked back in horror.

"And you never do get all the way rid of it. Spend time with that nightmare, and you can always see yourself in other people's eyes. Even now, people look at me and think I shouldn't wear a red coat and an orange dress, and I say to myself, 'Hey, I don't care what they think as long as they don't think it in my dreams.'"

"But it's only ever bad things. Why not any good things?" Kevin pleaded.

The woman shrugged. "That's why it's a nightmare."

She looked at Kevin sadly. "Better you than me," she said. Then she walked away, and this time Kevin didn't follow.

His thoughts ran through his head in circles. Six years. I'll be old. Six years, and she only got rid of it because she ran into an idiot like me. How many people that stupid can there be in the world? What if I never get rid of it? What if all the people in the world who are stupid enough to ask have already had it once and I was the very last dummy? Kevin had heard that there's a sucker born every minute. Maybe the next sucker was just being born, and Kevin would have to wait until he or she grew up enough to say, "Hey, gimme that nightmare. It's just what I always wanted."

Kevin went home. He ate his supper without a word and headed to his room to do his homework. His mother looked with concern at the dark circles under his eyes, but Kevin was too steeped in misery to care. That night he turned a resigned face to the dream mirrors. The woman in the red coat didn't appear, but the disgust of the manager at Orly's oozed over Kevin and stuck like tar.

The next day was Monday. Kevin had run out of open doors at school, so he was forced to begin the cycle again with the main entrance and hope the high-school boys had forgotten him. As he rounded that corner from sunlight to shade, he was momentarily blinded. Shadow figures knocked his books out of his hands and pushed him against the wall.

"Hey, Kev," said a voice out of the dark, "you haven't been in the yard lately. We missed you."

Hunching his shoulders, Kevin could only think of how this scene would reappear in miserable dreams. He didn't really pay attention to what the older boy was saying.

"We were beginning to think you didn't like us, Kev. You do still like us, don't you?"

"Huh? Oh, yeah, sure."

"Doesn't sound real sincere. Tell you what, why don't you give us a token of your esteem?"

"What?"

The older boy held out his hand. "Hand it over, Kevin. Empty those pockets. Whatever you got, I want."

"You want . . . ?" He stopped in confusion and then was tongue-tied with rage. That was his chance. Maybe the only chance he'd ever have and he'd blown it. Now the boy leaned closer. He was going to ask again, but this time he would be specific. He wanted Kevin's lunch money, and Kevin was going to have the nightmare for the rest of his life. Kevin wanted to bang his own head against the wall he was so frustrated, but then, to Kevin's relief, the older boy repeated himself.

"Whatever you got, Kevin, I want. Do you understand?" He clenched his hand into a fist, then opened it again, palm up.

"Yeah," said Kevin, "yeah, sure." He cupped his hand around invisible Jell-O and tossed it into the older boy's waiting hand. "It's all yours," he said, and ran for the school doors as the bell rang.

Raymond's Run

by Toni Cade Bambara

Squeaky—also known as Hazel Elizabeth Deborah Parker—is responsible for her brother Raymond. She also likes to run and to win races in her New York City neighborhood. Since she knows how important it is to be respected, she wants to help Raymond find his own way to win respect.

I don't have much work to do around the house like some girls. My mother does that. And I don't have to earn my pocket money by hustling; George runs errands for the big boys and sells Christmas cards. And anything else that's got to get done, my father does. All I have to do in life is mind my brother Raymond, which is enough.

Sometimes I slip and say my little brother Raymond. But as any fool can see he's much bigger and he's older too. But a lot of people call him my little brother cause he needs looking after cause he's not quite right. And a lot of smart mouths got lots to say about that too, especially when George was minding him. But now, if anybody has anything to say to Raymond, anything to say about his big head, they have to come by me. And I don't play the dozens or believe in standing around with somebody in my face doing a lot of talking. I much rather just knock you down and take my chances even if I am a little girl with skinny arms and a squeaky voice, which is how I got the name Squeaky. And if things get too rough, I run. And as anybody can tell you, I'm the fastest thing on two feet.

There is no track meet that I don't win the first place medal. I use to win the 20-yard dash when I was a little kid in kindergarten. Nowadays it's the 50-yard dash. And tomorrow I'm subject to run the quarter-meter relay all by myself and come in first, second, and third. The big kids call me Mercury cause I'm the swiftest thing in the neighborhood. Everybody knows that—except two people who know better, my father and me.

He can beat me to Amsterdam Avenue with me having a two fire-hydrant headstart and him running with his hands in his pockets and whistling. But that's private information. Cause can you imagine some 35-year-old man stuffing himself into PAL shorts to race little kids? So as far as everyone's concerned, I'm the fastest and that goes for Gretchen, too, who has put out the tale that she is going to win the first place medal this year. Ridiculous. In the second place, she's got short legs. In the third place, she's got freckles. In the first place, no one can beat me and that's all there is to it.

I'm standing on the corner admiring the weather and about to take a stroll down Broadway so I can practice my breathing exercises, and I've got Raymond walking on the inside close to the buildings cause he's subject to fits of fantasy and starts thinking he's a circus per-former and that the curb is a tightrope strung high in the air. And sometimes after a rain, he likes to step down off his tightrope right into the gutter and slosh around getting his shoes and cuffs wet. Then I get hit when I get home. Or sometimes if you don't watch him, he'll dash across traffic to the island in the middle of Broadway and give the pigeons a fit. Then I have to go behind him apologizing to all the old people sitting around trying to get some sun and getting all upset with the pigeons fluttering around them, scattering their newspapers and upsetting the wax-paper lunches in their laps. So I keep Raymond on the inside of me, and he plays like he's driving a stage coach which is okay by me so long as he doesn't run me over or interrupt my breathing exercises, which I have to do on account of I'm serious about my running and don't care who knows it.

Now some people like to act like things come easy to them, won't let on that they practice. Not me. I'll high prance down 34th Street like a rodeo pony to keep my knees strong even if it does get my mother uptight so that she walks ahead like she's not with me, don't know me, is all by herself on a shopping trip, and I am somebody else's crazy child.

Now you take Cynthia Procter for instance. She's just the opposite. If there's a test tomorrow, she'll say something like, "Oh I guess I'll play handball this afternoon and watch television tonight," just to let you know she ain't thinking about the test. Or like last week when she won the spelling bee for the millionth time, "A good thing you got 'receive,' Squeaky, cause I would have got it wrong. I completely forgot about the spelling bee." And she'll clutch the lace on her blouse like it was a narrow escape. Oh, brother.

But of course when I pass her house on my early morning trots around the block, she is practicing the scales on the piano over and over and over and over. Then in music class, she always lets herself get bumped around so she falls accidentally on purpose onto the piano stool and is so surprised to find herself sitting there, and so decides just for fun to try out the ole keys and what do you know—Chopin's waltzes just spring out of her fingertips and she's the most surprised thing in the world. A regular prodigy. I could kill people like that.

I stay up all night studying the words for the spelling bee. And you can see me anytime of day practicing running. I never walk if I can trot and shame on Raymond if he can't keep up. But of course he does, cause if he hangs back someone's liable to walk up to him and get smart, or take his allowance from him, or ask him where he got that great big pumpkin head. People are so stupid sometimes.

So I'm strolling down Broadway breathing out and breathing in on counts of seven, which is my lucky number, and here comes Gretchen and her sidekicks—Mary Louise who used to be a friend of mine when she first moved to Harlem from Baltimore and got beat up by everybody till I took up for her on account of her mother and my mother used to sing in the same choir when they were young girls, but people ain't grateful, so now she hangs out with the new girl Gretchen and talks about me like a dog; and Rosie who is as fat as I am skinny and has a big mouth where Raymond is concerned and is too stupid to know that there is not a big deal of difference between herself and Raymond and that she can't afford to throw stones. So they are steady coming up Broadway and I see right away that it's going to be one of those Dodge City scenes cause the street ain't that big and they're close to the buildings just as we are. First I think I'll step into the candy store and look over the new comics and let them pass. But that's chicken and I've got a reputation to consider. So then I think I'll just walk straight on through them or over them if necessary. But as they get to me, they slow down. I'm ready to fight, cause like I said I don't feature a whole lot of chitchat, I much prefer to just knock you down right from the jump and save everybody a lotta precious time.

"You signing up for the May Day races?" smiles Mary Louise, only it's not a smile at all.

A dumb question like that doesn't deserve an answer. Besides, there's just me and Gretchen standing there really, so no use wasting my breath talking to shadows.

"I don't think you're going to win this time," says Rosie, trying to signify with her hands on her hips all salty, completely forgetting that I have whupped her behind many times for less salt than that.

"I always win cause I'm the best," I say straight at Gretchen who is, as far as I'm concerned, the only one talking in this ventriloquist-dummy routine.

Gretchen smiles but it's not a smile and I'm thinking that girls never really smile at each other because they don't know how and don't want to know how and there's probably no one to teach us how cause grown-up girls don't know either. Then they all look at Raymond who has just brought his mule team to a standstill. And they're about to see what trouble they can get into through him.

"What grade you in now, Raymond?"

"You got anything to say to my brother, you say it to me, Mary Louise Williams of Raggedy Town, Baltimore."

"What are you, his mother?" sasses Rosie.

"That's right, Fatso. And the next word out of anybody and I'll be their mother too." So they just stand there and Gretchen shifts from one leg to the other and so do they. Then Gretchen puts her hands on her hips and is about to say something with her freckle-face self but doesn't. Then she walks around me looking me up and down but keeps walking up Broadway, and her sidekicks follow her. So me and Raymond smile at each other and he says "Giddyap" to his team and I continue with my breathing exercises, strolling down Broadway toward the icey man on 145th with not a care in the world cause I am Miss Quicksilver herself.

I take my time getting to the park on May Day because the track meet is the last thing on the program. The biggest thing on the program is the May Pole dancing which I can do without, thank you, even if my mother thinks it's a shame I don't take part and act like a girl for a change. You'd think my mother'd be grateful not to have to make me a white organdy dress with a big satin sash and buy me new white babydoll shoes that can't be taken out of the box till the big day. You'd think she'd be glad her daughter ain't out there prancing around a May Pole getting the new clothes all dirty and sweaty and trying to act like a fairy or a flower or whatever you're supposed to be when you should be trying to be yourself, whatever that is, which is, as far as I am concerned, a poor Black girl who really can't afford to buy shoes and a new dress you only wear once a lifetime cause it won't fit next year.

I was once a strawberry in a Hansel and Gretel pageant when I was in nursery school and didn't have no better sense than to dance on tiptoe with my arms in a circle over my head doing umbrella steps and being a perfect fool just so my mother and father could come dressed up and clap. You'd think they'd know better than to encourage that kind of nonsense. I am not a strawberry. I do not dance on my toes. I run. That is what I am all about. So I always come late to the May Day program, just in time to get my number pinned on and lay in the grass till they announce the 50-yard dash.

I put Raymond in the little swings, which is a tight squeeze this year and will be impossible next year. Then I look around for Mr. Pearson who pins the numbers on. I'm really looking for Gretchen if you want to know the truth, but she's not around. The park is jam-packed. Parents in hats and corsages and breast-pocket handkerchiefs peeking up. Kids in white dresses and light blue suits. The parkees unfolding chairs and chasing the rowdy kids from Lenox as if they had no right to be there. The big guys with their caps on backwards, leaning against the fence swirling the basketballs on the tips of their fingers waiting for all these crazy people to clear out the park so they can play. Most of the kids in my class are carrying bass drums and glockenspiels and flutes. You'd think they'd put in a few bongos or something for real like that.

Then here comes Mr. Pearson with his clipboard and his cards and pencils and whistles and safety pins and 50 million other things he's always dropping all over the place with his clumsy self. He sticks out in a crowd cause he's on stilts. We used to call him Jack and the Beanstalk to get him mad. But I'm the only one that can outrun him and get away, and I'm too grown for that silliness now.

"Well, Squeaky," he says, checking my name off the list and handing me number seven and two pins. And I'm thinking he's got no right to call me Squeaky if I can't call him Beanstalk.

"Hazel Elizabeth Deborah Parker," I correct him and tell him to write it down on his board.

"Well, Hazel Elizabeth Deborah Parker, going to give someone else a break this year?" I squint at him real hard to see if he is seriously thinking I should lose the race on purpose just to give someone else a break.

"Only six girls running this time," he continues, shaking his head sadly like it's my fault all of New York didn't turn out in sneakers. "That new girl should give you a run for your money." He looks around the park for Gretchen like a periscope in a submarine movie. "Wouldn't it be a nice gesture if you were . . . to ahhh . . . ."

I give him such a look he couldn't finish putting that idea into words. Grownups got a lot of nerve sometimes. I pin number seven to myself and stomp away, I'm so burnt. And I go straight for the track and stretch out on the grass while the band winds up with "Oh the Monkey Wrapped His Tail Around the Flag Pole," which my teacher calls by some other name. The man on the loudspeaker is calling everyone over to the track and I'm on my back looking at the sky trying to pretend I'm in the country, but I can't, because even grass in the city feels hard as sidewalk and there's just no pretending you are anywhere but in a "concrete jungle" as my grandfather says.

The 20-yard dash takes all of the two minutes cause most of the little kids don't know no better than to run off the track or run the wrong way or run smack into the fence and fall down and cry. One little kid though has got the good sense to run straight for the white ribbon up ahead so he wins. Then the second graders line up for the 30-yard dash and I don't even bother to turn my head to watch cause Raphael Perez always wins. He wins before he even begins by psyching the runners, telling them they're going to trip on their shoelaces and fall on their faces or lose their shorts or something, which he doesn't really have to do since he is very fast, almost as fast as I am. After that is the 40-yard dash which I use to run when I was in first grade. Raymond is hollering from the swings cause he knows I'm about to do my thing cause the man on the loudspeaker has just announced the 50-yard dash, although he might just as well be giving a recipe for Angel Food cake cause you can hardly make out what he's saying for the static. I get up and slip off my sweat pants and then I see Gretchen standing at the starting line kicking her legs out like a pro. Then as I get into place I see that ole Raymond is in line on the other side of the fence, bending down with his fingers on the ground just like he knew what he was doing. I was going to yell at him but then I didn't. It burns up your energy to holler.

Every time, just before I take off in a race, I always feel like I'm in a dream, the kind of dream you have when you're sick with fever and feel all hot and weightless. I dream I'm flying over a sandy beach in the early morning sun, kissing the leaves of the trees as I fly by. And there's always the smell of apples, just like in the country when I was little and use to think I was a choo-choo train, running through the fields of corn and chugging up the hill to the orchard. And all the time I'm dreaming this, I get lighter and lighter until I'm flying over the beach again, getting blown through the sky like a feather that weighs nothing at all. But once I spread my fingers in the dirt and crouch over for the Get On Your Mark, the dream goes and I am solid again and am telling myself, Squeaky you must win, you must win, you are the fastest thing in the world, you can even beat your father up Amsterdam if you really try. And then I feel my weight coming back just behind my knees then down to my feet then into the earth and the pistol shot explodes in my blood and I am off and weightless again, flying past the other runners, my arms pumping up and down and the whole world is quiet except for the crunch as I zoom over the gravel in the track. I glance to my left and there is no one. To the right a blurred Gretchen who's got her chin jutting out as if it would win the race all by itself. And on the other side of the fence is Raymond with his arms down to his side and the palms tucked up behind him, running, in his very own style and the first time I ever saw that and I almost stop to watch my brother Raymond on his first run. But the white ribbon is bouncing toward me and I tear past it racing into the distance till my feet with a mind of their own start digging up footfuls of dirt and brake me short. Then all the kids standing on the side pile on me, banging me on the back and slapping my head with their May Day programs, for I have won again and everybody on 151st Street can walk tall for another year.

"In first place . . . ." the man on the loudspeaker is clear as a bell now. But then he pauses and the loudspeaker starts to whine. Then static. And I lean down to catch my breath and here comes Gretchen walking back for she's overshot the finish line too, huffing and puffing with her hands on her hips taking it slow, breathing in steady time like a real pro and I sort of like her a little for the first time. "In first place . . . ." and then three or four voices get all mixed up on the loudspeaker and I dig my sneaker into the grass and stare at Gretchen who's staring back, we both wondering just who did win. I can hear old Beanstalk arguing with the man on the loudspeaker and then a few others running their mouths about what the stop watches say.

Then I hear Raymond yanking at the fence to call me and I wave to shush him, but he keeps rattling the fence like a gorilla in a cage like in them gorilla movies, but then like a dancer or something he starts climbing up nice and easy but very fast. And it occurs to me, watching how smoothly he climbs hand over hand and remembering how he looked running with his arms down to his side and with the wind pulling his mouth back and his teeth showing and all, it occurred to me that Raymond would make a very fine runner. Doesn't he always keep up with me on my trots? And he surely knows how to breathe in counts of seven cause he's always doing it at the dinner table, which drives my brother George up the wall. And I'm smiling to beat the band cause if I've lost this race, or if me and Gretchen tied, or even if I've won, I can always retire as a runner and begin a whole new career as a coach with Raymond as my champion. After all, with a little more study I can beat Cynthia and her phony self at the spelling bee. And if I bugged my mother, I could get piano lessons and become a star. And I have a big rep as the baddest thing around. And I've got a roomful of ribbons and medals and awards. But what has Raymond got to call his own?

So I stand there with my new plan, laughing out loud by this time as Raymond jumps down from the fence and runs over with his teeth showing and his arms down to the side which no one before him has quite mastered as a running style. And by the time he comes over I'm jumping up and down so glad to see him—my brother Raymond, a great runner in the family tradition. But of course everyone thinks I'm jumping up and down because the men on the loudspeaker have finally gotten themselves together and compared notes and are announcing "In first place—Miss Hazel Elizabeth Deborah Parker." (Dig that.) In second place—Miss Gretchen P. Lewis." And I look over at Gretchen wondering what the P stands for. And I smile. Cause she's good, no doubt about it. Maybe she'd like to help me coach Raymond; she obviously is serious about running, as any fool can see. And she nods to congratulate me and then she smiles. And I smile. We stand there with this big smile of respect between us. It's about as real a smile as girls can do for each other, considering we don't practice real smiling every day you know, cause maybe we too busy being flowers or fairies or strawberries instead of something honest and worthy of respect . . . you know . . . like being people.

Making a Fist

by Naomi Shihab Nye

"We forget that we are all dead men conversing with dead men."

—*Jorge Luis Borges*

For the first time, on the road north of Tampico,
I felt the life sliding out of me,
a drum in the desert, harder and harder to hear.
I was seven, I lay in the car
watching palm trees swirl a sickening pattern past the glass.
My stomach was a melon split wide inside my skin.

"How do you know if you are going to die?"
I begged my mother.
We had been traveling for days.
With strange confidence she answered,
"When you can no longer make a fist."

Years later I smile to think of that journey,
the borders we must cross separately,
stamped with our unanswerable woes.
I who did not die, who am still living,
still lying in the backseat behind all my questions,
clenching and opening one small hand.

Harry Sloan

by T. Pat Matthews & Claude V. Dunnagan

*During the Depression of the 1930s, writers were
enrolled in a government program to provide work for
the unemployed. Under the Federal Writers' Project—for
a salary of about $20 a week—writers interviewed
people throughout the nation and wrote their stories in
their own words. This is the true account of a white
farmer in North Carolina.*

Pa was a tenant farmer, just like I am now. Ma and the girls
tended the house and the garden, while pa and us boys worked
the tobacco. We generally had plenty to eat—roasting ears and
string beans and Irish potatoes and okra and collards and turnip
greens in summer, and grits and cane syrup and fresh hog meat in
winter. We bought green coffee in the bulk and roasted it—only Ma
kept a package of Arbuckle brand for when the preacher came. On
Sundays we had fried chicken, especially if there was company.

None of us children got no education to speak of. There wasn't no
compulsory law then to make us go to school. Sometimes now I wish
there had been. I can read printing a little but I can't read writing, and
I never was no good at figuring. We went for a couple of seasons to a
little one-room school two miles from home. A funny thing happened
once. The teacher had just give me a whuppin for talking too much,

and I was feeling powerful bad, and mean, too. On the way home a toad-frog came a-hoppin across the road, just as happy and careless. I couldn't stand to see him looking so pert—so I took a big rock and mashed him out flat. "You won't hop no more," I says.

Just then Bud Seegars come up behind me and says, "Good Lord, boy, didn't you know it's bad luck to kill a toad-frog? It'll make the cow dry up every time, or maybe die. You watch."

When I got home I seen my daddy a-runnin out to the barn with a big long-necked bottle in his hand. The old cow was a-lying on the ground, all bloated up, and pa was pouring a dose of castor oil and turpentine down her throat. "She bust into the clover patch and foundered," he says. I didn't say nothin. That night the old cow died. Pa kept complaining about the green clover a-killing her, and I never did tell him no better. He woulda just a-give me another whuppin.

Our church was named Welcome Home Church, and it was set way back in a shady grove. In the cool of the evening we'd load up the mule wagon with straw, and all pile in and drive along the sandy road. Then we'd git out and hitch and talk to our friends a few minutes. At the church door the men and women would separate and set on opposite sides of the house. There was lots of babies, and in one corner at the back a bunch of quilts was put on the floor and the babies laid down to sleep till the meeting was over. There wasn't no light but a couple of kerosene lamps, and it was right hard to pick out the right baby when the meeting broke up. Old Jim Vincent over here has complained all his life about not really being a Vincent—says he was swapped off at a revival meeting when he was a baby.

People know'd how to sing in them days, and the preacher know'd how to preach. He showed us hell on one side and heaven on the other, and there warn't no middle ground. We had to make up our minds, one way or the other.

After the meeting had run about two weeks, there'd be a big baptizing in the creek. The preacher would have on a long black coat and wade out to his waist in the muddy water. He'd poke around with his walking-cane to see there wasn't no roots or stumps for nobody to get hurt on. Then he'd stand there in the water and tell how John the Baptist baptized Jesus, and how there wasn't no other way to salvation. The converts was all lined up on the bank, about 40 or 50 of em. The girls was dressed in white and looked kind of scared.

Then the crowd would sing, "Shall we gather at the river, the beautiful, the beautiful river," and the line would move down into the water. The girls' dresses would float up around their waists, and the preacher would poke em down with his cane. He'd lay his hands on each one and say, "I baptize thee in the name of the Father and the Son and the Holy Ghost, amen," and then he'd dip em over backward into the water. As they come up, he'd pat each one on the shoulder and say, "Sister, you're saved." The girls would come up on the bank all dripping wet, and the women would throw a cloak around em and take em off somewhere and dress em in dry clothes.

That's the way I happened to marry Sally. We was converted at the same meeting and baptized at the same baptizing. When she come up out of the water, all shivering and blue around the lips, I know'd right then I wanted to marry her. She was 16 and I was 19, and her folks didn't make no objection. We rented a little place back in the Blue Creek district, and I got a job sawmilling. I got 50 cents a day, and it was pretty hard getting along. Sally had a baby that year, and by spring the mill had cut all the timber out and I lost my job. Then I rented another place and went to tobacco farming on the shares.

Tending five acres of tobacco is hard work for one man and a mule, especially when you got a landlord like I had. His name was Harold Kimzey. He advanced credit for fertilizer and stuff and charged me ten percent interest. When it wasn't paid on time, he added 20 percent more. At the end of the year we had a little trouble. We had a record of all our dealings, with the date of everything on it. Sally kept the figures and she's good at it. Come settling time, by the landlord's figures, all the crops was his and we still owed him. Our figures showed he owed us. We got a third party to help us, and we found we had a lot of the crop to our part. Mr. Kimzey had took our peas and all our corn, but when the mistake was found we got our 12 bushels of peas and 20 barrels of corn back. But Kimzey was mad, and he turned us out of the house on January first with no meat or other provisions except the peas and corn. We went from one landlord to another, and each one was worse than the last.

Then I rented a farm from H.K. Fettor, the best man I ever farmed with. His land wasn't much good, but he treated us right. By that time I had six children and seven dogs. Some of the children was big enough to work, and we put in 14 hours a day in the field. When the tobacco was being barned and graded, we put in 18. I worked myself sick and didn't make nothing much. I decided it wasn't no use, and went to hunting with dogs and getting drunk. Seem like it was all the pleasure I had.

One Saturday night I come home pretty well filled with liquor, and I was mighty cold. Sally and all the children had gone to bed, and the house was dark. I saw a few coals in the fireplace, and got down on my knees to blow em into a flame. I blowed and blowed, but nothing happened. Then I seen I was just blowin at a patch of moonlight that come through the window and fell on the ashes. I got up and tried to go to bed, but the bed was going round and round, and I couldn't catch up with it. So I just stood by the door and waited for it to come around to me. Every time the bed would come around I'd make a jump for it, and every time I jumped I'd hit the floor, kerplunk. Sally woke up and got me onto the bed and took off my shoes and covered me up. This oughta broke me from drinking, but it didn't.

I reckon we've got along pretty well, considering everything. If it wasn't for careless, mean landlords and low tobacco prices, a tenant farmer could make out. Most of the houses we've lived in have been in bad shape—glass broke out and half the windows boarded up. If the roof leaks the tenant has to fix it himself—no use waiting for the landlord to do it. We've never had electricity, nor any water except a well. I never heard of a telephone in a tenant house—but we wouldn't have no use for one anyway.

The worst trouble is never knowing what you're going to do next. A farmer never knows what his tobacco will bring. There ain't no regular market price like there is for cotton. There's a hundred different kinds of tobacco, and the farmer's always got the wrong kind to fetch a good price. The buyers know what they're doing, and the warehousemen know, but the farmer don't know nothing. He has to take what he can get and be thankful he ain't starving. I don't believe nobody knows what the auctioneer says. It's just a lot of stuff got up to fool people.

When I first started out I hoped to buy a farm sometime, but I soon saw I couldn't do this, so I give up the idea. My next aim was to have a good pack of hounds and some good guns. I have them. Best of all, I've raised my children to be respectable. I've got 10, which is one short of what my daddy done, but Sally says she don't care if it is. Her

health ain't what it once was, and she has to take medicine for female trouble. But we have a happy home, plenty of dogs, stock, and farming tools, and we are satisfied and happy.

The Big Deal

by Paddy Chayefsky

In the early days of television, plays were performed "live" for broadcast. Settings were simple, since film was not used. In this play from the 1950s, Joe Manx has to decide who he is and what he wants. We usually think of young people making these decisions—but the story of Joe, a man in his 50s, shows that older people can be faced with the same questions.

CHARACTERS

JOE MANX
THE WIFE
THE DAUGHTER
HARRY GERBER
DAUGHERTY
GEORGE
THE COMPLAINER
THE WELL-DRESSED MAN
SAM HARVARD
CONSTRUCTION MEN

FADE IN: *Interior restaurant—not too posh, but the tables have linen tablecloths. Camera wends its way between two*

78

tables at which various chatting people are eating their luncheon. A waiter and a couple crowd their way past camera. General effect of crowded café.

We narrow our attention to a little man of 50-odd years seated at a table, studying a cup of coffee in front of him. He has on a blue pencil-stripe suit, single-breasted, and which somehow gives the feeling of the 1930's. His tie is tied into a narrow, elegant knot; but it is slightly askew. His shirt collar turns up at the edges. His fedora rests on the table at his elbow. This is Joe Manx. He looks up, and his face perks up a bit as he recognizes someone approaching his table. A moment later a pretty girl of 26 comes to his table . . . bends over him, gives him a quick kiss.

THE DAUGHTER: Hello, Pa.

JOE: Sit down, Marilyn, sit down. You want something to eat? Eggs, a sandwich, anything like that?

THE DAUGHTER [*sitting*]: No, Pa, I'm meeting George for lunch in about 15 minutes.

JOE: Sure. Give him my regards when you see him. I won't hold you. I happen to need about 10, 15 dollars if you happen to have it on you.

THE DAUGHTER [*promptly opening her purse*]: Sure, Pa.

JOE: I ran across a very interesting proposition today, and I'd like to take the man out for a couple of drinks. I have an appointment with him at four o'clock.

THE DAUGHTER [*extracting some bills from her purse*]: Are you sure 15 bucks will be enough?

JOE: Oh, plenty, plenty. I'm just going to take him for a couple of drinks. [*Takes the bills*] I might be able to pay you this back on Thursday, because I'm playing a little pinochle over at Harry Gerber's tomorrow night, and I usually come out a couple of bucks ahead. Listen, Marilyn, don't let me hold you. I know you're anxious to get to see George.

THE DAUGHTER: All right, Pa. I'll see you later.

JOE: Just let me say that this is a very interesting proposition that I ran across today. I don't want to sound premature, but I have a feeling that this might be the deal I've been looking for. I won't bore you with the details. I only want to say this proposition involves Louie Miles, if the name is at all familiar to you. He happens to be one of the biggest

79

contractors in the business. Eighteen years ago, he was a lousy little plasterer. I gave him his first work. Well, I was down the Municipal Building today. It happened that I . . . . Well, look, I don't want to hold you. I can see you're anxious to see your boyfriend. Go ahead, go ahead. Give him my regards. Don't tell your mother you gave me some money.

THE DAUGHTER [*who has been smiling fondly at her father throughout his speech*]: Okay, Pa, I'll see you.

JOE: I'll see you. I'll see you. Have a good lunch.

> [THE DAUGHTER *exits off.* JOE *sits a moment, fingering the two bills his daughter has just given him. Then he suddenly lifts a hand imperiously and calls sharply out.*]

JOE: Waiter! Check!

> DISSOLVE TO: *A section of one of those little restaurants you always find around hospitals. We see two booths . . . . Camera dollies past first booth, which contains two young doctors, one middle-aged doctor, and a young nurse—all in traditional white hospital uniforms.*

> *We move in on second booth, which contains* THE DAUGHTER *and a young resident doctor named* GEORGE. *He is wearing the conventional white-jacketed uniform, with innumerable pencils and pens clipped into his outer breast pocket. They have their pie and coffee in front of them—also the dishes of the meal they have just eaten, which have not been taken away yet.* THE DAUGHTER *is eating her pie, but* GEORGE *is just fiddling with his fork. They are both obviously caught in deep discussion.*

THE DAUGHTER: I know these aren't ideal circumstances to get married in, but who gets married in ideal circumstances? Do you know what I mean?

GEORGE: I know, I know.

THE DAUGHTER: I mean, everybody has problems when they get married. They got parents to support, and finding a place to live, and they don't have enough money. These are just things everybody has to face when they get married. Look at Alex and Ann Macy. Neither of them had a job when they got married. We're lucky compared to them, for heaven's sakes.

GEORGE: Well, what do you want to do? You want to get married then?

THE DAUGHTER: Yeah.

GEORGE: Well, let's get married then. Let's get it over with.

THE DAUGHTER: Let's get it over with. You make it sound like I was going to electrocute you.

GEORGE: Look, Marilyn, marriage is a responsible business. I've got two more years of residency. You're going to have to support me for two years. That's the trouble with being a doctor. The first half of his life he has to be supported by somebody. It's a terrible thing to feel that somebody is sacrificing for you all the time. My mother and father, they went through torture to make me a doctor. Every time my old man sends me a check, I get a little sick in my stomach. And they don't understand, you know what I mean. They don't understand why I just don't rent myself an office on Halsey Street and open up a practice. I finished my year of interning. I'm an M.D. They don't understand why I'm taking all these years of residency at a salary of 22 dollars a month . . . . Well, I want to be an internist, that's why. I like internal medicine. I don't want to be a G.P. There's a thousand G.P.'s on Halsey Street now. Every ground-floor window you walk by, there's another G.P.

THE DAUGHTER: George . . . .

GEORGE: Well, the point is, Marilyn, I've got two more years of residency ahead of me, and you're going to have to support me for two years.

THE DAUGHTER: I'm making a good salary, George.

GEORGE: You're already supporting your mother and father.

THE DAUGHTER: I've got the five thousand dollars my Aunt Eva left me.

GEORGE: Look, Marilyn, you want to get married, it's all right with me. Let's get married. [THE DAUGHTER *frowns down at her plate.*] I mean it. I'm not on call tomorrow. We'll go down to City Hall and get married. What do we need, blood tests? All right, I'll take you up to the blood lab right now—finish your coffee—we'll go up to the blood lab and we'll get our specimens taken. What do we have to wait, three days? What's today, Tuesday? All right, we'll get married on Friday. [*They both look down at their plates. A moment of uncomfortable silence.*] My mother is dead set against this marriage, you know that, don't you? Even my old man, who likes you a lot, says I can't afford to take on a wife at this moment.

THE DAUGHTER: Take on a wife! What am I, some kind of a bundle you're going to carry on your back?

GEORGE: I didn't mean it that way.

THE DAUGHTER: You're a boy, you know that? You're a 17-year-old boy. What do you think marriage is? Death in a gas chamber? Marriage is making somebody happy. You get better from marriage, not worse. Maybe you might find the next two years a little easier if you had somebody near you who wants you to be happy with all her heart and soul. [THE DAUGHTER'*s eyes are wet with tears now.*] I want you to be an internist! I want you to finish your residency! I don't care if I have to support half of Toledo, Ohio! It's no sacrifice to me if it makes you happy! And I expect the same from you!

> [*She hides her eyes in her hand and tries to master herself.* GEORGE *sits in the sudden vacuum left by* THE DAUGHTER'*s outburst, looking down at his hands folded in his lap. Then he looks up and across at his girl friend and smiles gently.*]

GEORGE [*rises—crosses around table—sits beside her*]: Marilyn, honestly, I don't know why I'm making such a crisis out of this. I'm a little scared, that's all. You just forget how much you love the girl. I would like to officially set our wedding for this coming Friday, if you'll have me, and I promise to make you happy. So what do you say?

THE DAUGHTER: I finally collared you, eh?

GEORGE [*beaming*]: Yeah.

> DISSOLVE TO: *The front hallway of a four-and-a-half room apartment. We are looking at the front door, which now opens and admits* JOE MANX. *He closes the door behind him, takes off his hat, puts it on the mail table. Then, carrying himself with a sort of bantam erectness, he passes into the living room. The camera ambles along after him.*
>
> *The living room is furnished with what had been good, solid, expensive middle-class furniture two decades ago. The dominating piece in the living room is a large dark mahogany table with thick, intricately carved legs. At the head of the table is a massive chair with thick armrests, obviously the chair of the master of the house. It is to this chair that Joe marches. He takes off his jacket, drapes it around the back of the chair, rolls up his shirt sleeves two turns, loosens his tie, unbuttons his collar, and then sits*

down in the chair, placing his arms on the armrests. For a
moment he just sits there, enjoying a small feeling of
majesty. Then he lifts his head and calls out.

JOE: I'm home!

[The W*ife appears in the kitchen doorway. She is a strong*
woman of about 50. She is dressed in a house dress and is
carrying a dish towel. On her face there is the anticipatory
smile of someone who is about to impart a secret. Her secret
becomes immediately apparent when The D*aughter*
appears behind her in the kitchen doorway.]

THE WIFE [*surveying her husband with that smile*]: Joe, I got
something in the nature of a pleasant shock to tell you, so get a good
hold on your chair. I don't want you to fall off and hit your head on
the floor.

[*She comes into the living room, takes a chair at the far end*
of the table.]

JOE: I ran across a very interesting proposition today.

THE DAUGHTER [*also sidling into the room, wearing a smile*]:
Hello, Pa.

JOE: I was down the Municipal Building. I was with Martin Kingsley.
Martin was having a little permit trouble, so he says to me: "Joe, come
on down with me to the Housing Department." After all,
Commissioner Gerber is a very good friend of mine. He figured I
might put in a couple of good words for him.

THE WIFE: Did you talk to Harry Gerber about that other matter?

JOE: Doris, I'm telling a story, don't interrupt. Well, all right, I went
down to the Municipal Building. I'm standing in the hallway by the
water fountain. I went over to get a drink . . . so . . . .

THE WIFE: Joe . . . .

JOE: A man comes over to me. A big fat bald-headed man. He looks at
me, he says: "Aren't you Joe Manx?" So I look at him, I say: "You'll have
to excuse me. Your face is familiar, but I can't quite place you." So he
looks at me, he says: "I'm Louie Miles!" Doris, you remember Louie
Miles? Seventeen, 18 years ago. He was a plasterer.

THE WIFE: Joe . . . .

JOE: It seems he's a big construction man now in Cleveland. Well,
that's neither here nor there. So anyway, we got to talking about
this and that and it seems that he's bought himself a piece of land,

about 15 acres, out near Willaston, with the intention of putting up 60 or 80 houses, small ranch houses, 15 thousand, maybe 16 tops. Well, he starts to dig a little, and Boom! He runs into water. I said to him: "Louie, for heaven's sakes, if you would have asked me, I would have told you. The whole Willaston area is nothing but marshland." Well, the upshot of it is, he wants to sell the land. We made a date for four o'clock at the Statler Hotel. [*Rises, crosses to his daughter*] Sweetheart, I wonder if you would do me a very big favor.

THE DAUGHTER: Sure, Pa.

JOE: I wonder if you could get me a small glass of cold water. I'm very thirsty.

THE DAUGHTER: Sure. [*She promptly exits into the kitchen.*]

JOE: Well, I began to do a little quick thinking. If I had 150 acres of that land, that's six million square feet . . . with a 50-foot frontage, I could put up a thousand houses. With a thousand houses, it's worth the trouble and expense of draining. *Now*, my dear lady, we are talking in terms of a million dollar proposition. One thousand small houses, nothing big, low-income houses, like that Levittown in New York . . . . Have you any idea how much money that man Levitt made? Countless millions! Countless! [THE DAUGHTER *returns with the glass of water, which she sets at her father's place.*] Thank you, sweetheart, thank you.

THE WIFE: Joe, Marilyn also ran across a very interesting proposition today.

JOE: The upshot of it all was, at four o'clock, I went to the Statler . . . . I said: "Louie, what do you think of *this* idea? Louie," I said, "why don't we buy up another 150, 160 more acres, and instead of setting up a lousy 60 houses, we'll set up a thousand!" Well, I'll tell you something. If you ever saw a man get shocked, you should have seen Louie Mile's face when I said that. He looked at me like I was crazy.

THE WIFE: He was right, too.

JOE: That's very funny. When I built those houses on Chestnut Street and Halsey Street and King Boulevard, everybody also looked at me like I was crazy.

THE WIFE: That was in 1934.

JOE: That whole Chestnut Street district was nothing but swamps. Snakes and frogs. The grass was so high you could get lost in it.

THE WIFE: All right, Joe, what was the upshot of it all with Louie Miles?

JOE: The upshot of it all was that he couldn't see it. He wants to sell that 15 acres. He wants to get out of the whole deal. So I said to him: "Louie, what do you want for that 15 acres?" So he says: "Four thousand dollars." So I said: "Louie, I may take that land right off your hands." And that's the way it stands at this moment.

THE WIFE: As long as you were down the Housing Department today, did you go in and see Harry Gerber?

[JOE *suddenly scowls.*]

JOE: Doris, I want to get one thing straight right now. I don't want to hear anything more about Harry Gerber. I don't need your advice and counsel. It seems to be your pleasure to make fun of me . . . .

THE WIFE: I don't make fun of you, Joe.

JOE: As far as you're concerned, I'm a big talker without a nickel to his name, who thinks he's a big shot. All right, I'm broke. I'm strapped. But I was once the biggest builder in this city, and I'm still a respected name in the trade. Go to Frank Daugherty and Sons. Mention the name of Joe Manx, see what he says. Deputy Housing Commissioner Harry Gerber still calls me up once or twice a week for a little advice. State Senator Howard Schram came halfway across a restaurant to ask my opinion about a bill he's pushing through up in Columbus. So when I tell you this is a million-dollar proposition don't be so clever. Don't be so smart. When I die, there will be a million dollars in my will, don't worry.

[*Returns to his master chair, sits down, disgruntled and scowling. An uncomfortable silence falls over the family. At last,* DAUGHTER *leans to her father.*]

THE DAUGHTER [*smiling*]: Pa, I'm getting married Friday.

[JOE *turns his head slowly and regards* THE DAUGHTER *with open-mouthed shock.*]

JOE: When did this happen?

THE DAUGHTER: Just at lunch, just after I saw you.

THE WIFE: I told you we had a shock for you.

JOE: Well, for heaven's sakes! Which one is this, the doctor? George? [THE DAUGHTER *nods her head happily.*] Well, where is he, for heaven's sakes? This calls for some kind of a celebration. Seems to me we should have some wine, a little festivity. For heaven's sakes! A man

85

comes walking home, and his daughter casually remarks, she's getting married! Listen, call him up on the phone, tell him to come over tonight . . . .

THE DAUGHTER [*smiling*]: He's on duty tonight, Pa.

JOE: I'm taking the whole bunch of us out for a real celebration.

THE DAUGHTER: He's coming over tomorrow night, Pa.

[JOE *is staring at his wife, who is beaming.*]

JOE: What are you sitting there in a house dress for? Your daughter's getting married. Go put some lipstick on, for heaven's sakes!

THE WIFE: I just found out myself 15 minutes ago.

THE DAUGHTER: Pa . . . .

JOE: What's the fanciest restaurant in town?

THE WIFE: I got chicken in the stove now.

JOE: We'll eat it cold tomorrow. [*He is herding his wife out of her chair.*] Come on. Into the bedroom. Put on a dress with feathers on it. Joe Manx's daughter gets married, this town is going to hear about it.

THE DAUGHTER [*laughing . . . to* THE WIFE, *who is being crowded to the door*]: All right, Ma. I feel like celebrating myself.

THE WIFE [*over her husband's shoulder to her daughter*]: Marilyn, do me a favor. Go in the kitchen, turn off all the fires.

THE DAUGHTER: Sure, Ma.

[THE WIFE *exits.* THE DAUGHTER *goes into the kitchen.* JOE *stands by the kitchen doorway.*]

JOE [*more or less to Marilyn in the kitchen*]: Well, this is certainly an occasion. A nice young fellow. He's going to make a success out of himself. In a couple of years, mark my words, he'll be making 20, 30 thousand bucks a year . . . . [*Crosses to the kitchen doorway and stands on the threshold watching his daughter.*] Under a little different circumstances, I would have given you two kids a wedding, the whole city of Toledo would talk about it for weeks. I'd have a thousand dollars' worth of cold cuts alone. You'd have some big shots at your wedding, believe me! State Senator Howard Schram would be there, I can tell you that. They'd pour the whisky out of barrels. The ball-room would be littered with drunks. Very important drunks. Men worth in the millions.

[THE DAUGHTER *joins him at the kitchen doorway and stands listening to him with a smile of deep fondness and understanding. For a moment* JOE *returns her gaze, obviously very fond of his daughter. Then his eyes drop.*]

JOE [*his voice lowered*]: Marilyn, I'll need a couple of bucks to cover the evening. It might come as much as 20, 25 dollars.

THE DAUGHTER [*smiling*]: Sure, Pa.

> [*She reaches out with her hand and lightly touches his face. Then she turns and moves to the dining room table, where her purse lies. Camera stays on* JOE *for close-up. His eyes are closed. He has to control himself, or else he would cry.*]

> DISSOLVE TO: JOE *and* DORIS MANX'*s bedroom late that night. Actually, we open up on* THE WIFE, *dressed now in an old batiste nightgown. She is standing by the window, applying lotion to her hands and looking down, watching the operation. Then she turns and looks over to her husband and then back again to her hands.*

> THE CAMERA *pans slowly to* JOE, *who is unbuttoning his shirt—also wrapped in his thoughts. The push and aggressiveness have gone from* Joe. *He seems tired and a little slumped.*

> THE WIFE *now shuffles down the aisle between the twin beds and perches on hers. She rubs the lotion into her hands, but it is clear that she is fishing for the best way to open the conversation.*

THE WIFE [*still looking down as she creams her hands*]: Joe, she's going to have to support her husband for a couple of years. She isn't going to be able to pay the rent on this house no more. Maybe, we're going to have to move. I don't know. But we're not taking another penny from that girl. Even with Eva's five thousand dollars, it's going to be hard enough on her as it is. [JOE *sits on the far end of his bed, his back to his wife, a little slumped.*] Harry Gerber says he has a job for you with the city. Why don't you at least go down and talk to him about it?

JOE [*mumbling*]: I'll see Harry tomorrow. We're playing pinochle tomorrow night at his house.

THE WIFE [*who didn't quite hear him*]: I'm sorry, Joe. I didn't hear what you said.

JOE [*a little louder*]: I said, I'll see Harry tomorrow night. We're playing pinochle at his house tomorrow night.

THE WIFE: All right, you'll see him tomorrow night.

> [*Having finished rubbing her hands, she brings her feet onto the bed and picks up a newspaper from the bed table between the beds and starts to read.*]

JOE [*muttering*]: If you want to know, I went to see Harry Gerber last week.

THE WIFE [*reading*]: What did you say, Joe?

> [JOE *rises.*]

JOE: I said, I went to see Harry Gerber last week, if you want to know the truth.

> [THE WIFE *looks up from her paper.*]

THE WIFE: When was this?

JOE: Last week some time. I don't know. Tuesday, Wednesday. What do you think, I don't want a decent job? You think I like being supported by my daughter? You don't think it hurts?

THE WIFE: So what happened with Harry Gerber?

JOE: It was some job he had for me. A building inspector. 36 hundred dollars a year. 36 hundred dollars. Newspaper money. I put Harry Gerber into business. He was a 75-dollar-a-week accountant. I took him in and made him a partner. He offers me a 36-hundred-dollar-a-year job. Now, he's a big shot. Deputy Housing Commissioner. I told him what he could do with his job.

> [THE WIFE, *unable to think of anything appropriate to say, looks back at her newspaper.*]

JOE [*crying out*]: I'm not a 36-hundred-dollar-a-year-man!

THE WIFE: All right, don't yell so loud. She'll hear you.

> [*She puts the newspaper down, sits up.* JOE *moves around to the inside of his bed, sits down on his bed, faces his wife.*]

JOE: Doris, I was a big operator at one time.

THE WIFE: That was 15 years ago, Joe . . . .

JOE: All right, the bottom fell out of the real-estate market. I went broke. All right. I still got it up here . . . . [*Indicates his head*] I can't think in terms of 36 hundred dollars a year. I'm not a candy store owner, keeping an eye on the kids so they won't steal the pennies off the newsstand. I'm a businessman . . . .

THE WIFE: Joe, how many businesses have you tried? You tried the trucking business. You tried the . . . .

JOE: I was out of my element. I'm a builder. This is my racket.

THE WIFE: I won't let you take any more money off that girl.

JOE: What do you want me to do? You want me to take this job as a lousy building inspector?

THE WIFE: Joe, don't talk so loud.

JOE: You want me to walk around with my hand out, waiting for a five-dollar pay-off? I won't do it. Some of the biggest men in the business are my friends.

THE WIFE: All right, Joe, sit down. Don't be so excited.

> [JOE, *who has risen from his bed, now sinks back, his breath coming heavily.*]

JOE [*looking down at his knees*]: Don't worry about me, Doris. We're not going to take another penny off that girl. If you don't think it sticks me in my heart to ask her for 10 dollars here, 15 dollars there, so I can play a little pinochle. Don't you think I have a little contempt for myself? I don't have to be reminded. I love that girl. What have I ever given her? I couldn't even afford to send her to a decent college. I haven't even got a life-insurance policy so that she could at least benefit from my death.

THE WIFE: Oh, for heaven's sakes, Joe, don't be so dramatic. We had money once, we don't have it any more. You've had a long time to get used to that fact.

JOE [*pounding the bed table*]: I'm going to leave that girl a million dollars in my will!

THE WIFE: Joe, what are you yelling about? Go wash yourself and let's go to bed. You're in one of your moods, and I don't want to argue with you.

JOE: Listen, Joe Manx may be broke. He may be strapped. But he's still got it up here.

THE WIFE: Thirty-six hundred dollars a year would suit us fine. What do we need more? We're getting on in years.

JOE: There's a million-dollar proposition in that Willaston land. A little manipulation, a little maneuvering, and a man who hasn't got a nickel rides around in a Cadillac. Right now all I need is four thousand dollars. I want to pick up Louie Miles's land. You gotta have a piece of land to start with. You can't build without land ....

> [JOE *has forgotten his wife as he gets involved in his manipulations. He begins to pace slow, measured strides up*

89

and down beside his bed, his hands behind his back.]

JOE: All right, four thousand dollars. That's not so hard. I'll walk into Frank Daugherty's office, I'll say: "I want four thousand dollars," and that's all there is to that . . . .

[THE WIFE, *long familiar with these mutterings of her husband, turns her bed lamp off, turns over on her side, and tries to go to sleep. The only light in the room now is the bed lamp over* JOE'*s bed.*]

JOE: But now comes the manipulation. One hundred and 50 acres, draining and construction costs the way they are today, it's going to run at least 200, 250 thousand dollars . . . .

[*He lies back on the bed now, his hands folded over his paunch, his eyes wide and glowing.*]

JOE: I'll have to have the land and at least 50 thousand dollars before I can go to the banks. I'll call Sam Harvard first thing in the morning. This is something that might interest him . . . .

THE CAMERA *begins to move up slowly onto his face as he lies there dreaming aloud.*

JOE: I could possibly realize 200 thousand dollars out of this. A very interesting proposition. A very interesting proposition . . . .

THE CAMERA *moves right into his eyes.*

FADE OUT.

ACT II

FADE IN: *Construction work going on in a city. A high wooden fence has been erected around the large corner area of the construction. Towering above the fence are the skeletal girders of the proposed building. Noise and sounds of construction.*

THE CAMERA *pans slowly across this view, up and onto a huge wooden sign on which is written:*

A NEW 12-STORY OFFICE BUILDING

WILL BE ERECTED ON THIS SITE—

TO BE COMPLETED SEPTEMBER 1953

FRANK DAUGHERTY AND SONS,

GENERAL CONTRACTORS.

CLOSE IN *on name of* DAUGHERTY.

CUT TO: *Interior, construction shack, crudely furnished. A wooden table, piled with papers and blueprints, a portable typewriter. A telephone. Coveralls hang from wall nails. On the wall an artist's conception of the proposed office building with Daugherty's name in bold printed letters at the bottom.*

Two men are in the shop, both in their 40s. Both are roughhewn types. Both wear baggy suits and hats, despite the fact that it is a July day. They are leaning over a large blueprint spread out on the table, muttering indistinctly to each other. Suddenly one bursts out.

THE FIRST MAN: So what are we gonna do with all those guys sittin' out there?

THE SECOND MAN: Nothin'. The reinforcement rods aren't here yet.

[*The two men return to the blueprint. There is a knock at the door.*]

THE SECOND MAN [*without looking up, barks out*]: Come in!

[*The door opens and* JOE MANX *comes in, dressed as he was in Act I. He closes the door behind him. Neither man looks at him.*]

THE SECOND MAN: I knew that Andy Constantino would never come up with those five-eighths rods. So he said he would. So I said, drop dead. Well, who's right now, you tell me. [*Turns to* JOE] Wadda you want, mister?

JOE: I'm waiting for Frank Daugherty.

THE SECOND MAN: Waddaya wanna see him about?

JOE: I have a personal matter I want to see him about.

THE SECOND MAN: You can't wait in here. Wait outside.

THE FIRST MAN [*looking out the little window*]: Here comes Frank.

THE SECOND MAN: Oh, he's gonna blow the roof off about those rods, boy. I told him yesterday, they ain't gonna be here, and he said .... [*The door opens and a tall, angular Irishman of about 50 comes in.*] Listen, Frank, the rods didn't come in yet. I gotta whole crew outside waiting to get started. You told me yesterday, get them ready for the morning ....

DAUGHERTY: Where's Andy?

THE SECOND MAN: I don't know. He ain't here yet either.

DAUGHERTY [*to* THE FIRST MAN]: Get Andy on the phone for me. [*to*

JOE] Hello, Manx. Wadda you want?

JOE: I'd like to have a couple of minutes alone with you.

DAUGHERTY: I ain't got time now, Manx.

> [JOE *looks at* DAUGHERTY, *then at the scowling faces of the other two men.*]

JOE: I need four thousand dollars, Daugherty. I got a very interesting proposition.

DAUGHERTY: What is it?

JOE: I can get a hold of a piece of land . . . .

DAUGHERTY: What land?

JOE: Fifteen acres out in the Willaston area.

DAUGHERTY: Not interested.

THE FIRST MAN [*on phone*]: Is Andy Constantino there?...Well, where is he? Get ahold of him, tell him Frank Daugherty wants to talk to him right away—[*To* DAUGHERTY, *as he hangs up*] He ain't there, Frank.

THE SECOND MAN: He's probably out trying to round up some rods now.

JOE: Daugherty, I know it's marshland. But if you think in terms of a thousand houses . . . .

DAUGHERTY: That land won't hold houses. Louie Miles was around here yesterday, trying to sell me that piece-a-land. I tell you what I told Louie. I tried to build in Willaston five years ago. I was knee-deep in water. I don't want no part of it. I'm not interested. [*He crosses to door.*] Are we gonna have to pay those men-a-yours while we're waiting for those rods?

THE SECOND MAN: Yeah.

DAUGHERTY: Call the union . . . . Manx, that land won't hold any kind of foundation. I told Louie Miles to try and sell it to the city. They're looking for some land to put up a community playground.

THE SECOND MAN [*on phone*]: Is Herbie Swanson there? Daugherty wants him.

DAUGHERTY: That land might hold some tennis courts, that's about all it's good for.

JOE: I think you're making a mistake, Daugherty.

DAUGHERTY: It won't be the first time. [*Takes the phone from* THE SECOND MAN] Have you got them yet? [*into the receiver*] Hello? Hello? This is Frank Daugherty. Who'm I talking to?

[THE CAMERA *moves onto* JOE MANX. *His face shows a mixture of envy for the activity going on around him and embarrassment at his futility in front of the other men. Over him comes* DAUGHERTY's *voice.*]

DAUGHERTY: Listen, Herbie, I got a crew of lathers here, but I can't use them for at least a couple of hours. Do I have to pay them? . . . Ah, come on, Herbie, for Pete's sakes. I can't afford to throw seven hundred dollars down the sewer. I'm doing this job close to the skin as it is . . . . [JOE *turns and starts out of the shack.*] Well, maybe, you can help me out this way. You know where I can get ahold of 14 hundred rods right away? . . . I already tried Constantino. He was supposed to have them here this morning . . . .

[JOE *exits, closing the door behind him.*]

DISSOLVE TO: *The restaurant of Act I, Scene I. Actually, we fade in on a short, stout little man of about 50, named* SAM HARVARD. *He is hunched over his coffee, which he sips slowly and methodically in between small pieces of Danish pastry. Once he looks quickly across the table to* JOE *and then back to the pastry in his hand. He chews.*

HARVARD [*without looking up*]: Joe, why do you always hit me for these interesting propositions of yours? Why don't you hit someone else for a change?

JOE: I came to you, Sam, because . . . .

HARVARD: You came to me four, five years ago with some lunatic proposition about going into the trucking line, and I gave you two thousand dollars then, which I knew was money out the window when I gave it to you. And wasn't there something once about a tool-and-die plant you wanted to invest in, another of your interesting propositions that cost me a thousand, I think. Joe, why don't you hit somebody else for a change?

JOE: Sam, I'm going to tell you the truth. I went to Daugherty. I went to Irving Stone. I went to J. C. Shirmer Incorporated. They're getting old. They only want sure-fire propositions. Office buildings. Government jobs. I didn't want to come to you, Sam. I'm very conscious of the money that I owe you.

HARVARD: Don't be so conscious. You don't have to pay me. I don't need the money. But Joe, don't ask me for another four thousand dollars for such a lunatic proposition as this thousand ranch houses in Willaston.

JOE: I just want to remind you, I built houses before. I'm not a baby in this game. Go walk in the Chestnut Street area. Before I poured a footing there, the whole area was snakes and frogs. The grass was so high you could get lost . . . .

> [HARVARD *breaks off another piece of Danish, looks up from under his heavy brows.*]

HARVARD: Joe, the answer is no.

> [*He sips his coffee and chews slowly and methodically. We fade out.*]

> DISSOLVE TO: *A clock sitting on the buffet chest in the Manx's dining alcove. A telephone is ringing.* THE WIFE *comes out of the kitchen to answer it. She wears what might be her best dress, but her sleeves are rolled up.*

THE WIFE: Hello? . . . Hello, Joe, how are you? Where have you been all day? . . . Oh, plenty of things have been happening here. You missed all the fun. The groom's father called up about four-thirty and invited us over to their house this afternoon . . . . Yeah, we just came back about ten minutes ago. Quite a pair of in-laws we've inherited . . . . The father is all right, but the mother is a real cold potato . . . . [THE DAUGHTER *enters the room.* THE WIFE *interrupts her phone conversation to speak to* THE DAUGHTER.] Marilyn, do me a favor. I started some water boiling for the vegetables. Put some salt in it. Then take the chicken out of the refrigerator . . . [THE DAUGHTER *nods and passes on into the kitchen.*] Well, Joe, when are you coming home? . . . Why not? . . . Don't talk so fast. I can't understand you . . . . Joe, did something happen today to upset you? You sound very depressed. Are you depressed? . . . How do you feel, Joe? You don't sound good to me. Maybe you better give up the card game tonight and come on home and get some rest . . . . All right, don't get angry . . . . all right, Joe, give me a call when you get to Harry Gerber's . . . good-by, Joe . . . . [*Hangs up. She turns from the phone, frowning.* THE DAUGHTER *comes out of the kitchen and sets a bowl of salad on the table.*] He's not coming home for dinner . . . so let's just have the chicken from yesterday, and the vegetables, is that all right with you?

THE DAUGHTER: That's fine with me.

[THE DAUGHTER *goes back into the kitchen.* THE WIFE, *still frowning, goes to the buffet chest, opens a drawer, and extracts some silverware. She starts setting two places, but her thoughts are elsewhere. She sits, brows knit in thought.* THE DAUGHTER *comes back from the kitchen with a cold roast chicken, two large plates, and some paper napkins, sets up places for her mother and herself.*]

THE WIFE: I'm worried about him. I'm worried about him because he's beginning to talk like a fool. Four, five years ago, you listen to his big propositions, and you say: "Well, maybe. Maybe, some of his old friends will help him out." But now, it seems to me, he's beginning to sound like a comic character. What do you think, Marilyn?

THE DAUGHTER: Oh, he'll be all right, Ma.

THE WIFE: Do you think so? I don't think so. I think something terrible is going to happen to him. He doesn't talk like a completely sensible person any more. I look at him sometimes; it seems to me he's in another world, dreaming.

[THE DAUGHTER *sits across from her mother, studies the dish before her.*]

THE DAUGHTER: He was a big shot once. He had a taste of what it was like. It's hard for a man of his age to adjust to new situations.

THE WIFE: It's not a new situation. It's 15 years old. He's got to understand that it's not important to be the Governor's best friend. He was like that as long as I've known him, even as a boy. He was always the big spender. Before we were married, he used to take me to the Hippodrome in New York City. At that time, the Hippodrome was the big date of all dates. They used to have big spectacles there, like circuses. It used to cost a dollar. In those days, a dollar was a dollar. He used to take me every week. I never knew where he got the money. He never had a job in his life. He was always in this business or that business. He was always what we used to call a sport. He was the first one in our whole crowd to have a car. I'll never forget. He came driving down the street, wobbling from one sidewalk to the other. He was a kind, generous man, your father. He had an open hand to everybody. You were too young then. You don't remember. The parties we used to give when we lived in the big house on Rogers Boulevard! Every Sunday, I tell you that house used to be filled till two, three o'clock in the morning. Well, we don't give

95

big parties any more. He'll have to change. Eat some cold chicken!

THE DAUGHTER: He's not going to change, Ma. Not at his age.

THE WIFE: He's got to go out and earn a living, Marilyn.

THE DAUGHTER: Ma, why talk foolish? He isn't going to go out and get a job. In the first place where's he going to get a job? Who's going to give it to him?

THE WIFE: Harry Gerber offered him a job.

THE DAUGHTER [*surprised*]: Oh, yeah? When was this?

THE WIFE: A couple of weeks ago. It's a small job, a building inspector. It would be fine for us. He don't want to take it.

THE DAUGHTER: Ma, don't push him. It isn't in him. He likes big things. It would kill him to be a little man. I know that you're probably nagging him to take this job. You're thinking what a burden you and Pop are on me, especially now I'm getting married. It's no burden. Believe me. I don't resent it.

THE WIFE: Marilyn, you're not going to support Joe and me any more.

THE DAUGHTER: Ma, I talked this all out with George long ago. I'm going to take a couple of thousand out of Aunt Eva's money, and we're going to put it down on a little house somewheres, probably out in Kingston, and you and Pop are going to live with us. George says it's perfectly okay with him . . . .

THE WIFE: You're 26 years old. It's time to have babies.

THE DAUGHTER: Sure, it's time to have babies. When a baby comes, we'll worry about it. Listen, Ma, you don't think George and I haven't discussed this a thousand times between us? But life doesn't dovetail so nicely . . . . Don't worry about us. We'll have plenty of babies. [*The doorbell rings.*] How much you want to bet that's George?

> [*She plucks a piece of chicken loose, rises, and goes to the door munching away.* THE WIFE *suddenly starts from her seat.*]

THE WIFE: Oh, for heaven's sakes, I forgot the vegetables. The water's probably all boiled out already.

> [*She hurries into the kitchen.* THE DAUGHTER *opens the door of the apartment. It is, indeed,* GEORGE *standing there.*]

THE DAUGHTER: I knew it was you.

GEORGE: I haven't seen you in an hour. I missed you. Well, what are you going to do?

THE DAUGHTER: Come on in. You want some cold chicken?

[GEORGE *comes in.* THE DAUGHTER *closes the door behind him.*]

GEORGE: Tell you the truth, I figured we might go to a restaurant tonight, have a celebration. Because you know what?

THE DAUGHTER: What?

GEORGE: My mother likes your mother.

THE DAUGHTER: Hallelujah. Come on in, sit down for a minute.

[*She leads him back to the dining table, where they take seats.* THE DAUGHTER *calls to her mother in the kitchen.*]

THE DAUGHTER: It's him again, Ma.

GEORGE [*calling*]: Hello, Mrs. Manx.

THE WIFE [*off in kitchen*]: Hello, George. Give him some chicken, Marilyn.

THE DAUGHTER [*calling to* THE WIFE]: We're going to go out and eat, Ma, if you'll excuse us.

THE WIFE [*in kitchen*]: Sure. Go ahead, go ahead. [*She appears in the kitchen doorway, holding a saucepan.*] I burned the vegetables anyway. Go on out. Have a good time.

[*Disappears back into the kitchen.* THE DAUGHTER *and* GEORGE *sit for a minute.*]

THE DAUGHTER: My father was offered a job.

[GEORGE *looks up vaguely.*]

GEORGE: Yeah?

THE DAUGHTER: Yeah. It would be nice, eh?

GEORGE: Sure. Is he going to take it?

[THE DAUGHTER *thinks awhile, then shakes her head.*]

THE DAUGHTER: I don't think so, George. But it would be nice, I could even quit my job after a year.

GEORGE [*smiles*]: Yeah. Well, what do you say? You want to go?

THE DAUGHTER: Is this dress okay?

GEORGE: Sure.

[*They both stand.* THE DAUGHTER *moves slowly to* GEORGE, *and for a moment they stand, hazily warm and comfortable in their communication. She looks softly at him.*]

THE DAUGHTER: Good-by, Ma.

THE WIFE: Good-by, Marilyn. Good-by, George. Have a nice time.

GEORGE: Good-by, Mrs. Manx.

[The young couple move into the foyer, open the door, and pass out into the outside hallway—closing the door after them. THE WIFE *stands unmoving, watching them, even for a long moment after the door has closed behind them. Then she moves slowly to the telephone table, sets the saucepan down, dials a number, and waits expressionlessly for an answer.]*

THE WIFE: Harry? Is this Harry Gerber? . . . Harry, this is Doris Manx. Listen, did I take you away from your dinner? . . . Harry, I'll tell you why I called. Joe says he's coming over to your house for cards tonight . . . . Yeah, well I'm a little worried about him, Harry. He called up from downtown, he sounded very depressed . . . . Harry, make him take the job . . . . I know, Harry, but please make him take the job . . . .

DISSOLVE TO: JOE MANX *leaning forward over a table, reaching for some cards in front of another player. The camera dollies back to show the pinochle game taking place in* HARRY GERBER*'s living room. Four men sit around the table. On* JOE*'s right sits* THE COMPLAINER, *and directly across the table from* JOE *sits* THE WELL-DRESSED MAN, *so named for reasons that will soon be obvious. On* JOE*'s left sits* HARRY GERBER, *a heavy-set sympathetic man of 50. The living room is comfortably furnished: in particular, an easy chair.* JOE *has apparently just won the last hand and is to deal the next.*

THE COMPLAINER [*leaning across to* GERBER]: Why did you play the king? You knew he was sitting there with a singleton ace? If you led the ace, I woulda put the king on . . . .

THE WELL-DRESSED MAN: All right, all right, how much did this hand cost me?

GERBER: Half a dollar.

[GERBER *and* THE WELL-DRESSED MAN *send half a dollar to* JOE*'s little pile of money.* JOE *is riffling the cards.* THE COMPLAINER *is still complaining to* GERBER.]

THE COMPLAINER: If you run the government, Harry, like you play pinochle, no wonder we're in the condition we're in. [*To* JOE] How much do I owe you, Joe?

JOE: Half a dollar.

THE COMPLAINER [*pushing two quarters over to* JOE]: I haven't won a hand all night, you know that? I get nothing but nines and jacks.

THE WELL-DRESSED MAN: So I was telling you, Harry, I went into this store, and I told the salesman: "Look, money is no object. I want a suit that will hold its shape in hot weather." So he takes out this bolt of cloth . . . .

> THE CAMERA *moves in on* JOE *as he riffles the cards. His eyes are down. He is obviously thinking of other things than the card game. Over close-up, we hear the others' voices.*

THE COMPLAINER: Right now, all I want out of life is to see one flush, preferably in spades.

THE WELL-DRESSED MAN: Harry, feel this cloth, will you? Have you any idea how much this suit cost me? 189 dollars . . . .

> [JOE *begins to deal out the cards, three at a time first round, then four at a time until the deck runs out.*]

THE COMPLAINER: Joe, are we or are we not old friends?

JOE: Sure.

THE COMPLAINER: Then, deal me a decent hand, will you?

THE WELL-DRESSED MAN: Joe, take a guess. How much do you think I paid for this suit? 189 dollars. It's a special cloth, imported from Egypt. They wear this kind of material in the desert.

THE COMPLAINER [*picking up his cards as they come in*]: Joe, what are you dealing me here? What are you trying to do, bankrupt me?

THE WELL-DRESSED MAN: This material is as light as paper, but it wears like iron . . . .

THE COMPLAINER [*leaning over and showing his cards to* JOE, *who, as dealer, does not play in the hand*]: Look what you gave me, will you? Do you see 50 points meld in this whole hand? [*To the others*] All right, all right, who bids?

THE WELL-DRESSED MAN: So, Joe, let me tell you about this suit. . . .

THE COMPLAINER: Harry, what do you say?

GERBER: Three hundred. . . .

THE WELL-DRESSED MAN: So, Joe, this suit, rain or shine, it holds its crease. It doesn't wrinkle. I could jump in the river and swim in it, it won't wrinkle. The only trouble is, it makes me sweat so much. I'll be honest with you. I don't know how they manage in Egypt with it.

99

THE COMPLAINER: Hey, Lewisohn, what do you say?

THE WELL-DRESSED MAN: What?

THE COMPLAINER: Pick up your cards, will you? Gerber says 300. It's up to you.

THE WELL-DRESSED MAN [*painfully picking up one card at a time*]: I was telling Joe about the suit.

THE COMPLAINER: Lewisohn, do me a favor. The next time you come for a pinochle game, come naked, will you?…

THE WELL-DRESSED MAN [*screwing up his face as he examines each card and puts it into place in his hand*]: Let's see, what have I got here?

> [*Silence descends over the cardplayers as they wait for* THE WELL-DRESSED MAN *to figure out his hand. In the silence,* JOE *leans forward, folds his hands on the table before him, and speaks quietly.*]

JOE: Listen. I need 4,000 dollars. Can you give it to me, you fellows?

THE COMPLAINER [*turning to him*]: What?

JOE [*to* THE COMPLAINER]: What do you say, Davis? We've been playing pinochle together 20 years almost. Will you lend me 4,000 dollars?

THE COMPLAINER [*a little nervously*]: Lend it! Another couple of hands, and you'll win it from me.

THE WELL-DRESSED MAN [*laying his cards down and turning to* JOE]: What do you need the money for, Joe? Are you in trouble?

JOE: I need it for a business proposition. I want to buy a piece of land.

THE WELL-DRESSED MAN [*picking up his cards again*]: Oh, land. Land I don't know anything about. If you were in some kind of trouble—if you needed an operation or if you wanted to pay off a mortgage, something like that, I might be able to dig up a couple of thousand for you. But land I'm not interested in . . . .[*Studies his cards again*] Let's see. What's the bid to me?

THE COMPLAINER [*with nervous embarrassment*]: Come on, come on. Let's play cards. Gerber said 300. What do you say, Lewisohn?

THE WELL-DRESSED MAN: Three hundred is good with me.

THE COMPLAINER: It's good with me too. You want it, Harry, or not?

> [GERBER *is regarding* JOE MANX *with concern.*]

GERBER: Joe, what is this proposition you want the 4,000 for?

[JOE, *in a sudden burst of irascibility, slams the table with his hand.*]

JOE [*almost snarling*]: Come on! Come on, Harry! Let's play cards! It's 300 up to you! Do you want it or not?

GERBER [*without even looking at his hand*]: I don't want it.

JOE: All right, throw in the hand. Here, deal. [*He pushes the discards, as they are thrown down, toward* GERBER.] Look. Are we going to play cards, or are we going to talk! If we're going to play, let's play! If we're going to talk, let's talk! [*He suddenly stands, growing more frenzied.*] My friends! My friends! My good friends! Four lousy thousand bucks! You can't lend me four lousy thousand bucks! What am I, some kind of a bum or something? I built plenty of houses in my time! Good double-brick houses, three coats of plaster! [*He seizes the few bills and silver in front of him and scatters the money on the table.*] Here! A couple more bucks for you!

[*He turns and walks out.* GERBER *rises quickly from his seat.*]

GERBER [*calling*]: Joe!

[*He moves quickly after his friend.*]

SLOW DISSOLVE TO: JOE MANX, *sitting in the easy chair in* GERBER's *living room. Some time has passed—about an hour. The overhead lights of the previous scene have been turned off, and now the only illumination comes from the standing lamp behind the easy chair. There is enough light to see, however, as we pull back, that the cards still lie scattered on the table—except for a few that* HARRY GERBER *is shuffling and reshuffling as he sits at the table. There is a cup of coffee in front of* HARRY GERBER, *and* JOE *is holding his cup, sipping occasionally. He appears to have calmed down a great deal, even to the point of depression.*

JOE: I went to them all, Harry. I went to Daugherty, to Shirmer. I went to Sam Harvard, Marty Kingsley, Irving Stone. Some of these men used to mix cement for me. I couldn't raise 4,000 dollars. I couldn't raise 4,000 dollars! Daugherty brushed me off him like I was mud on his pants. I tell you, Harry, if somebody told me yesterday that Joe Manx couldn't raise 4,000 dollars, I would have laughed in his face. What does it mean, will you tell me? What does it mean?

GERBER: Joe….

101

JOE: Tell me the truth, Harry, do they laugh at me when I'm not around?

GERBER: All right, I'll tell you the truth. You haven't got a name in this trade any more, Joe, and you're kidding yourself if you think you have. You can go on like this the rest of your life, or you can act like a *mensch* and face a couple of facts. I got a job for you. Come and take it. It's the best job I can get for you. I tried to get you a desk job where you could feel like an executive, but the flat truth is they wouldn't have you. I'm leveling with you, Joe. Take it or leave it. It's 36 hundred dollars a year. It'll pay your rent, and it'll give you a little self-respect. [*Turns his attention back to the few cards he is shuffling.*] Joe, I'm your friend. Any time you need me, you know you can come to me. If I had 4,000 dollars, I'd give it to you. But I want you to know I'd give it to you out of charity, and I'd never expect to see it again.

JOE [*studying his coffee*]: Well, that's straight talk. I respect you for it. But I don't want your job.

[*He sets the coffee down on an end table.*]

GERBER: What is it, a question of pride? Are you ashamed to work for me?

JOE [*stands*]: Harry, I've been a bankrupt for 15 years. When you're a bankrupt as long as I am, 36 hundred dollars a year ain't gonna turn the trick. It isn't going to make up for all the failures.

GERBER: What failures?

JOE: You talk about facing facts! All right, let's face some facts! I failed as a man! I failed as a father! What did I ever give those two women?! What did I ever give them?! My wife wears the same cloth coat for four years, do you know that?

GERBER: You haven't failed anybody, Joe.

JOE: From the age of ten I never bought my daughter even a birthday present! She's getting married Friday. What will my wedding gift be? A house for the newlyweds? A 10,000-dollar bond? Do you know how it haunts me that I can't buy that girl something? What contempt she must have for me!

GERBER: Joe, you're talking like a fool. You're a wonderful father. Your girl is crazy about you. Stop torturing yourself.

JOE: Look, Harry, don't worry about me. I'm having a little rough time right now, but I'll come out of it. I'm 52 years old. Maybe I can't run around the block any more, but I'm still operating where it counts.

GERBER: Joe, sit down a minute.

JOE: Apparently, nobody has any faith in me, not even my best friend. Well, Harry, I'll dig up 4,000 dollars somewhere, one way or another, and I'll buy 15 lousy acres of swamp .... [*His voice is beginning to rise.*] And I'll show you what Joe Manx can do with it! I'll put the Empire State Building on that swamp! I'm a man of respect! Bricklayers like Frank Daugherty will come on their knees to kiss my hand! [*He suddenly smiles, but there is something almost wild about him.*] And, Harry, when I die, I'll leave 36 hundred dollars a year for you in my will.

> [*He nods his head once or twice—then turns and stumps out of the room.*]

FADE OUT.

ACT III

FADE IN: *The bedroom of* JOE *and* DORIS MANX, *later that night. The room is dark. We fade in on* THE WIFE, *lying on her back on her bed, asleep. Suddenly her eyes open. Then her head slowly turns in the direction of her husband's bed. The camera slowly pans over to* JOE's *bed. It is empty. The blankets have been pushed aside, and the sheets are mussed—indicating that* JOE *has recently been sleeping there.*

> THE WIFE *slowly sits up in bed, tense and apprehensive, but outwardly expressionless. She moves quickly around the beds to the door of the bedroom, opens it, passes into the dark hallway. She goes through the kitchen, opens that door, and steps into the living room.*

> JOE MANX *is seated in his large master chair, his arms resting regally on the armrests. He wears his trousers and bedroom slippers, but he has no shirt on. His hair is uncombed, and there is a distraught quality about him.*

THE WIFE: What's the matter, Joe? You can't sleep?

> [JOE *regards his wife with wide eyes.*]

JOE: Doris, I'll tell you what I've been thinking. I think I'm going to go away for a couple of days. I just called the station. I can get a train to Saint Louis at 4:49 A.M. Then I catch a flyer for Las Vegas. [*Stands, begins to pace around, hands behind his back*]...the convention

103

last year in Atlantic City—a feller there from Las Vegas. He told me, Las Vegas is just booming. He says, houses are springing up overnight. A city jumping up out of the desert. Like Florida in the 1920s. Well, I think I'll take a look at this Las Vegas. Listen, a clever man can make himself a bundle. [*He's patting his pants pockets for cigarettes now.*] Then too, I might have a look in California, see what the situation on the Coast is. Listen, I've heard wonderful things about the Coast. Los Angeles, San Diego. I've got some friends in San Diego. They told me: "Manx, any time you feel like switching your area of activity, there's plenty of room for you here."

THE WIFE: Joe, come to bed.

[JOE *comes to the table, leans intently across to his wife.*]

JOE: Lady, I have a feeling Las Vegas is going to turn the trick. I was lying in bed thinking, and then, suddenly—like the burning bush—it came to me. It was like somebody spoke the thought aloud. "Go to Las Vegas." What am I pushing pennies in Toledo? Well, let's pack up a couple of things for me and a toothbrush.

[*He starts briskly past his wife for the kitchen door, but his wife puts out a gentle hand on his forearm.*]

THE WIFE: Joe….

[*Her touch seems to crumble him. He turns to her, suddenly gaunt and broken.*]

JOE [*crying out in sheer anguish*]: Doris! I gotta get outta this town!

THE WIFE: I know, Joe, I know….

JOE: They're squeezing me here! You understand?! They're squeezing me!

THE WIFE: I understand, Joe.

JOE: Look at me, for heaven's sakes. They all make a living but me. What's the matter with me?

THE WIFE: There's nothing the matter with you, Joe.

[*He crosses to sofa, sits, slack and empty.*]

JOE: I would just like to close my eyes and wake up with another name, because I'm sick in my heart of being Joe Manx.

THE WIFE: Joe, we don't want a million dollars from you. We love you, Joe, we love you if you build houses or if you don't build houses. We just want to have you around the house. We like to eat dinner with you. We like to see your face.

[JOE *rises heavily from his seat and moves a few paces away. As he moves from* THE WIFE, *he lets his hand rest lightly against her face in mute appreciation of her sympathy.* THE WIFE *sits there, deeply weary herself.*]

JOE [*muttering*]: I don't know, maybe there's something in this Las Vegas.

THE WIFE [*more sharply than she intended*]: There's nothing in Las Vegas, Joe! [*She sits, trying to hold the edge of impatience inside of her, fishing desperately in her mind for something to say to her husband.*] Joe, I'm tired myself. I'd like to have a little peace. I'd like to know we live in a certain place and that a certain amount of money is coming in every week, so at least we know where we stand. I don't want a lot of money. I just don't want to have to carry a sick feeling in my stomach all the time that you're going to come home depressed and miserable. I don't want to listen to you turning around in bed all night long. I want to be able to go to sleep peacefully, knowing that you're also having a good night's sleep. I don't have much strength left, Joe. This kind of living is eating us up.

[*Deeply exhausted, she rests her face in the palm of one hand.* JOE *stands silently. She has reached home with him. Finally he comes to her and gently takes her arm.*]

JOE: It's all right, Doris, it's all right. Go to sleep.

THE WIFE [*still hiding her face in her hand*]: You owe this to me, Joe.

JOE [*helps her from the chair*]: Go to sleep. I want to do a little thinking.

THE WIFE: Joe, if I said anything that hurt you, it's because I'm all knocked out.

JOE [*helping her to the door*]: You didn't hurt me.

THE WIFE: Let's go to bed. We'll get some sleep.

JOE: Go to sleep, Doris. You're all knocked out. I'm going to work out something, don't worry. [*They stand now on the kitchen threshold, looking wearily at each other.*] I don't deserve you, Doris.

THE WIFE: Come to bed, Joe.

JOE: In a couple of minutes.

[THE WIFE *turns and shuffles out of view.* JOE *watches her disappearing form for a few moments. Then he turns and begins again the slow measured pacing up and down the dining room. We stay with him for four or five lengths of the room.*]

FADE OUT SLOWLY.

DISSOLVE TO: *Close-up of daughter's face. She is sleeping. We are in her bedroom, which is just off the living room. It is dark.* THE DAUGHTER *turns in her bed and then reverts back to her original position. Then—somehow aware that she is being looked at—she opens her eyes and awakens. She looks up.* JOE *is standing beside her bed, looking down at her. She is up on her elbow immediately.*]

THE DAUGHTER: Is something wrong, Pa?

JOE [*in a low voice*]: I wonder if I could talk to you for a minute, Marilyn.

THE DAUGHTER: Sure.

JOE: Listen, Marilyn, I'm going to ask a terrific favor of you . . . .

THE DAUGHTER: Sure, Pa . . . .

JOE: First let me finish. I need your 5,000 dollars. I want to buy Louie Miles's land. It's the only piece of land I can get my hands on, do you understand? Its a piece of swamp. It's marsh. But it's the best I can get. I have to have land before I can manipulate. I know what it means to you, Marilyn, the 5,000 dollars. I know you need it for your marriage. But you have to have faith in me. I'll give it back to you a thousand times over, Marilyn, I wouldn't ask you this, but I need it.

THE DAUGHTER: Sure, Pa. I'll made you out a check now. You can cash it in the morning.

[*She starts to sit up.* JOE *stares at her, unbelieving. Then the accumulated tension breaks within him, and he begins to sob. He turns away from his daughter in shame and goes out into the living room, hiding his eyes in his hands, the sobs coming in hoarse, half-caught gasps. He walks aimlessly around the living room, hiding his eyes, crying uncontrollably. His daughter appears in the doorway of her room, watching him anxiously.*]

THE DAUGHTER: Pa . . . .

[*He turns to her, still hiding his eyes.*]

JOE [*brokenly*]: What did I ever give you?

[*He sinks down onto a chair, cupping his face in both hands now.* THE DAUGHTER *moves slowly to him.*]

THE DAUGHTER: Pa, look at me. Am I an unhappy girl? I'm happy. I love George. I love you. I love Mama. I got a responsible job. The boss is satisfied with me. That's what you gave me. I'll make you out the check.

> [JOE *has to shake his head a few times before he can answer.*]

JOE: I don't want it.

> [*He rises weakly and starts for the kitchen door.*]

THE DAUGHTER: Pa....

JOE: Go to sleep, go to sleep....

> [*He goes into the kitchen, across it, and down the foyer to the door of his bedroom, opens it, and goes in. His wife is lying on her bed and turns to watch his entrance. He doesn't look at her. He goes to his bed, sits down. He is over his tears now and is just breathing heavily.*]

JOE [*mumbling*]: All right, all right. I'll take the job with Harry Gerber.

THE WIFE: I didn't hear you, Joe.

JOE [*louder*]: I said, I'll take the job with Harry Gerber. At least, they'll have one honest building inspector. [*He lies back on the bed now, looking up at the ceiling.*] This was a crazy day, a crazy day ....

> [*His eyes close and he dozes off.*]
>
> FADE OUT.

The Winter Hibiscus

by Minfong Ho

It's not easy to decide how to fit in the society around you. It seems especially difficult for Saeng, whose family has come so far from their homeland of Laos.

Saeng stood in the open doorway and shivered as a gust of wind swept past, sending a swirl of red maple leaves rustling against her legs. Early October, and already the trees were being stripped bare. A leaf brushed against Saeng's sleeve, and she snatched at it, briefly admiring the web of dark veins against the fiery red, before letting it go again, to be carried off by the wind.

Last year she had so many maple leaves pressed between the pages of her thick algebra textbook that her teacher had suggested gently that she transfer the leaves to some other books at home. Instead, Saeng had simply taken the carefully pressed leaves out and left them in a pile in her room, where they moldered, turned smelly, and were eventually tossed out. Saeng had felt a vague regret, but no anger.

For a moment Saeng stood on the doorstep and watched the swirl of autumn leaves in the afternoon sunlight, thinking of the bleak winter ahead. She had lived through enough of them now to dread their grayness and silence and endless bone-chilling cold. She buttoned up her coat and walked down the worn path through their yard and toward the sidewalk.

"Bai sai?" her mother called to her, straightening up from neat rows of hot peppers and snow peas that were growing in the vacant lot next door.

"To take my driving test," Saeng replied in English.

Saeng remembered enough Laotian to understand just about everything that her parents said to her, but she felt more comfortable now speaking in English. In the four years since they had migrated to America, they had evolved a kind of bilingual dialogue, where her parents would continue to address her brothers and her in Laotian, and they would reply in English, with each side sometimes slipping into the other's language to convey certain key words that seemed impossible to translate.

"Luuke ji fao bai hed yang?" her mother asked.

"There's no rush," Saeng conceded. "I just want to get there in plenty of time."

"You'll get there much too soon, and then what? You'll just stand around fretting and making yourself tense," Mrs. Panouvong continued in Laotian. "Better that you should help me harvest some of these melons."

Saeng hesitated. How could she explain to her mother that she wanted to just "hang out" with the other schoolmates who were scheduled to take the test that afternoon, and to savor the tingle of anticipation when David Lambert would drive up in his old blue Chevy and hand her the car keys?

"The last of the hot peppers should be picked, and the kale covered with a layer of mulch," Mrs. Panouvong added, wiping one hand across her shirt and leaving a streak of mud there.

Saeng glanced down at her own clean clothes. She had dressed carefully for the test—and for David. She had on a gray wool skirt and a Fair Isles sweater, both courtesy of David's mother from their last rummage sale at the church. And she had combed out her long black hair and left it hanging straight down her back the way she had seen the blond cheerleaders do theirs, instead of bunching it up with a rubber band.

109

"Come help your mother a little. *Mahteh, luuke*—Come on, child," her mother said gently.

There were certain words that held a strange resonance for Saeng, as if there were whispered echoes behind them. *Luuke,* or child, was one of these words. When her mother called her *luuke* in that soft, teasing way, Saeng could hear the voices of her grandmother, and her uncle, or her primary-school teachers behind it, as if there were an invisible chorus of smiling adults calling her, chiding her.

"Just for a while," Saeng said, and walked over to the melons, careful not to get her skirt tangled in any vines.

Together they worked in companionable silence for some time. The frost had already killed the snow peas and Chinese cabbage, and Saeng helped pluck out the limp brown stems and leaves. But the bitter melons, knobby and green, were still intact and ready to be harvested. Her mother had been insistent on planting only vegetables that weren't readily available at the local supermarkets, sending away for seeds from various Chinatowns as far away as New York and San Francisco. At first alone, then joined by the rest of her family, she had hoed the hard dirt of the vacant lot behind their dilapidated old house and planted the seeds in neat rows.

That first summer, their family had also gone smelting every night while the vast schools of fish were swimming upriver to spawn and had caught enough to fill their freezer full of smelt. And at dawn, when the dew was still thick on the grass, they had also combed the golf course at the country club for nightcrawlers, filling up large buckets with worms that they would sell later to the roadside grocery stores as fishbait. The money from selling the worms enabled them to by a hundred-pound sack of the best long-grain fragrant rice, and that, together with the frozen smelt and homegrown vegetables, had lasted them through most of their first winter.

"America has opened her doors to us as guests," Saeng's mother had said. "We don't want to sit around waiting for its handouts like beggars." She and Mr. Panouvong had swallowed their pride and gotten jobs as a dishwasher and a janitor, and they were taking English lessons at night under a state program that, to their amazement, actually paid them for studying!

By the end of their second year, they were off welfare and were saving up for a cheap secondhand car, something that they could never have been able to afford as grade-school teachers back in Laos.

And Saeng, their oldest child, had been designated their family driver.

"So you will be taking the driving test in the Lambert car?" Mrs. Panouvong asked now, adeptly twisting tiny hot peppers from their stems.

Saeng nodded. "Not their big station wagon, but the small blue car—David's." There it was again, that flutter of excitement as she said David's name. And yet he had hardly spoken to her more than two or three times, and each time only at the specific request of his mother.

Mrs. Lambert—their sponsor into the United States—was a large, genial woman with a ready smile and two brown braids wreathed around her head. The wife of the Lutheran minister in their town, she had already helped sponsor two Laotian refugee families and seemed to have enough energy and good will to sponsor several more. Four years ago, when they had first arrived, it was she who had taken the Panouvong family on their rounds of medical check-ups, social welfare interviews, school enrollments, and housing applications.

And it was Mrs. Lambert who had suggested, after Saeng had finished her driver-education course, that she use David's car to take her driving test. Cheerfully, David—a senior on the school basketball team—had driven Saeng around and taken her for a few test runs in his car to familiarize her with it. Exciting times they might have been for Saeng—it was the closest she had ever come to being on a date— but for David it was just something he was doing out of deference to his mother. Saeng had no illusions about this. Nor did she really mind it. It was enough for her at this point just to vaguely pretend at dating. At 16, she did not really feel ready for some of the things most 13-year-olds in America seemed to be doing. Even watching MTV sometimes made her wince in embarrassment.

"He's a good boy, David is," Saeng's mother said, as if echoing Saeng's thoughts. "Listens to his mother and father." She poured the hot peppers from her cupped palm to a woven basket and looked at Saeng. "How are you going to thank him for letting you use his car and everything?"

Saeng considered this. "I'll say thank you, I guess. Isn't that enough?"

"I think not. Why don't you buy for him a Big Mac?" Big Mac was one of the few English words Mrs. Panouvong would say, pronouncing it *Bee-Maag*. Ever since her husband had taken them to a McDonald's as a treat after his first pay raise, she had thought of Big Macs as the epitome of everything American.

To her daughter's surprise, she fished out a 20-dollar bill from her coat pocket now and held it out to Saeng. "You can buy yourself one too. A Bee-Maag."

Saeng did not know what to say. Here was a woman so frugal that she had insisted on taking home her containers after her McDonald's meal, suddenly handing out 20 dollars for two "children" to splurge on.

"Take it, child," Mrs. Panouvong said. "Now go—you don't want to be late for your test." She smiled. "How nice it'll be when you drive us to work. Think of all the time we'll save. And the bus fares."

The money, tucked safely away in her coat pocket, seemed to keep Saeng warm on her walk across town to the site of the driving test.

She reached it a few minutes early and stood on the corner, glancing around her. There were a few other teenagers waiting on the sidewalk or sitting on the hoods of their cars, but David was nowhere in sight. On the opposite side of the street was the McDonald's restaurant, and for a moment she imagined how it would be to have David and her sitting at one of the window seats, facing each other, in satisfyingly full view of all the passersby.

A light honk brought her back to reality. David cruised by, waving at her from his car window. He parallel parked the car, with an effortless swerve that Saeng admired, and got out.

"Ready?" David asked, eyebrow arched quizzically as he handed her his car keys.

Saeng nodded. Her mouth suddenly felt dry, and she licked her lips.

"Don't forget: step on the gas real gently. You don't want to jerk the car forward the way you did last time," David said with a grin.

"I won't," Saeng said, and managed a smile.

Another car drove up, and the test instructor stepped out of it and onto the curb in front of them. He was a pale, overweight man whose thick lips jutted out from behind a bushy moustache. On his paunch was balanced a clipboard which he was busy marking.

Finally he looked up and saw Saeng. "Miss Saeng Panouvong?"

he asked, slurring the name so much that Saeng did not recognize it as her own until she felt David nudge her slightly.

"Y—yes, sir," Saeng answered.

"Your turn. Get in."

Then Saeng was behind the wheel, the paunchy man seated next to her, clipboard on his lap.

"Drive to the end of the street and take a right," the test instructor said. He spoke in a low, bored staccato that Saeng had to strain to understand.

Obediently, she started up the car, careful to step on the accelerator very slowly, and eased the car out into the middle of the street. *Check the rearview mirror, make the hand gestures, take a deep breath,* Saeng told herself.

So far, so good. At the intersection at the end of the street, she slowed down. Two cars were coming down the cross street toward her at quite a high speed. Instinctively, she stopped and waited for them both to drive past. Instead, they both stopped, as if waiting for her to proceed.

Saeng hesitated. Should she go ahead and take the turn before them or wait until they went past?

Better to be cautious, she decided and waited, switching gears over to neutral.

For what seemed an interminable moment, nobody moved. Then the other cars went through the intersection, one after the other. Carefully, Saeng then took her turn *(turn signal, hand signal, look both ways).*

As she continued to drive down the street, out of the corner of her eye she saw the instructor mark down something on his clipboard.

A mistake, she thought. *He's writing down a mistake I just made. But what did I do wrong?* She stole a quick look at his face. It was stern but impassive. *Maybe I should ask him right now, what I did wrong,* Saeng wondered.

"Watch out!" he suddenly exclaimed. "That's a stop sign!"

Startled, Saeng jerked the car to a stop—but not soon enough. They were right in the middle of the crossroads.

The instructor shook his head. An almost imperceptible gesture, but Saeng noted it with a sinking feeling in her stomach.

"Back up," he snapped.

Her heart beating hard, Saeng managed to reverse the car and back up to the stop sign that she had just gone through.

"You might as well go back to where we started out," the instructor said. "Take a right here, and another right at the next intersection."

It's over, Saeng thought. He doesn't even want to see me go up the hill or parallel park or anything. I've failed.

Swallowing hard, she managed to drive the rest of the way back. In the distance she could see the big M archway outside the McDonald's restaurant, and as she approached, she noticed David standing on the opposite curb, hands on his hips, watching their approach.

With gratitude she noticed that he had somehow managed to stake out two parking spaces in a row so that she could have plenty of space to swerve into place.

She breathed a deep sigh of relief when the car was safely parked. Only after she had turned off the ignition did she dare look the instructor in the face.

"How—how did I do, sir?" she asked him, hating the quaver in her own voice.

"You'll get your results in the mail next week," he said in that bored monotone again, as if he had parroted the same sentence countless times. Then he must have seen the anxious, pleading look on Saeng's face, for he seemed to soften somewhat. "You stopped when you didn't need to—you had right of way at that first intersection," he said. "Then at the second intersection, when you should have stopped at the stop sign, you went right through it." He shrugged. "Too bad," he mumbled.

Then he was out of the car, clipboard and all, and strolling down the curb to the next car.

It had all happened so quickly. Saeng felt limp. So she had failed. She felt a burning shame sting her cheeks. She had never failed a test before. Not even when she had first arrived in school and had not understood a word the teacher had said, had she ever failed a test.

Tests, always tests—there had been so many tests in the last four years. Math tests, spelling tests, science tests, and for each one she had prepared herself, learned what was expected of her, steeled herself, taken the test, and somehow passed. She thought of the long evenings she had spent at the kitchen table after the dinner dishes had been cleared away, when she and her mother had used their battered English-Lao dictionary to look up virtually every single word in her textbooks and carefully written the Lao equivalent above the English word, so that there were faint spidery pencil marks filling up all the spaces between the lines of her textbooks.

All those tests behind her, and now she had failed. Failed the one test that might have enabled her to help her parents get to work more easily, save them some money, and earn her some status among her classmates.

David's face appeared at the window. "How'd it go?" he asked with his usual cheerful grin.

Saeng suppressed an urge to pass her hand over his mouth and wipe the grin off. "Not so good," she said. She started to explain, then gave it up. It wasn't worth the effort, and besides, he didn't really care anyway.

He was holding the car door open for her and seemed a little impatient for her to get out. Saeng squirmed out of the seat, then remembered the 20-dollar bill her mother had given her.

"Eh . . . thanks," she murmured awkwardly as she got out of the car. "It was nice of you to come here. And letting me use your car."

"Don't mention it," he said, sliding into the driver's seat already and pushing it back several inches.

"Would you . . . I mean, if you'd like, I could buy. . . ." Saeng faltered as she saw that David wasn't even listening to her. His attention had been distracted by someone waving to him from across the street. He was waving back and smiling. Saeng followed the direction of his glance and saw a tall girl in tight jeans and a flannel shirt standing just under the *M* archway. Someone blond and vivacious, her dimpled smile revealing two rows of dazzling white, regimentally straight teeth. Definitely a cheerleader, Saeng decided.

"Hold on, I'll be right with you," David was calling over to her. Abruptly he pulled the car door shut, flashed Saeng a perfunctory smile, and started to drive off. "Better luck next time," he said as his car pulled away, leaving her standing in the middle of the road.

Saeng watched him make a fluid U-turn and pull up right next to the tall blond girl, who swung herself gracefully into the seat next to David. For a moment they sat there laughing and talking in the car. So carefree, so casual—so American. They reminded Saeng of the Ken and Barbie dolls that she had stared at with such

115

curiosity and longing when she had first arrived in the country.

But it wasn't even longing or envy that she felt now, Saeng realized. This girl could have been David's twin sister, and Saeng would still have felt this stab of pain, this recognition that They Belonged, and she didn't.

Another car drove slowly past her, and she caught a glimpse of her reflection on its window. Her arms were hanging limply by her sides, and she looked short and frumpy. Her hair was disheveled and her clothes seemed drab and old-fashioned—exactly as if they had come out of a rummage sale. She looked wrong. Totally out of place.

"Hey, move it! You're blocking traffic."

A car had pulled up alongside of her, and in the front passenger seat sat the test instructor scowling at her, his thick lips taut with irritation.

Saeng stood rooted to the spot. She stared at him, stared at those thick lips beneath the bushy moustache. And suddenly she was jolted back to another time, another place, another voice—it had all been so long ago, and so far away, yet now she still found herself immobilized by the immediacy of the past.

Once, shortly after she had arrived in America, when she had been watching an absorbing ballet program on the PBS channel at Mrs. Lambert's house, someone had switched channels with a remote control, and it seemed as if the gracefully dying Odette in *Swan Lake* had suddenly been riddled with bullets from a screeching getaway car. So jarring had it been that Saeng felt as if an electric shock had charged through her, jolting her from one reality into another.

It was like that now, as if someone had switched channels in her life. She was no longer standing on a quiet street in downtown Danby but in the midst of a jostling crowd of tired, dusty people under a blazing sun. And it was not the balding driving instructor yelling at her, but a thick-lipped man in a khaki uniform, waving at them imperiously with a submachine gun.

Ban Vinai, Thailand. 1978. Things clicked into place, but it was no use knowing the name and number of the channel. The fear and dread still suffused her. She still felt like the scared, bone-weary little girl she had been then, being herded into the barbed-wire fencing of the refugee camp after they had escaped across the Mekong River from Laos.

"What're you doing, standing in the middle of the road? Get out of the way!"

And click—the Thai soldier was the test instructor again. Saeng blinked, blinked away the fear and fatigue of that memory, and slowly that old reality receded. In a daze she turned and made her way over to the curb, stepped up onto it, and started walking away.

Breathe deep, don't break down, she told herself fiercely. She could imagine David and that cheerleader staring at her behind her back. *I am tough,* she thought, *I am strong, I can take it.*

The sidewalk was littered with little acorns, and she kicked at them viciously as she walked and walked.

Only when she had turned the corner and was safely out of sight of David and the others did she finally stop. She found herself standing under a huge tree whose widespread branches were now almost leafless. An acorn dropped down and hit her on the head, before bouncing off into the street.

It seemed like the final indignity. Angrily, Saeng reached up for the branch directly overhead and tore off some of the large brown leaves still left. They were dry and crisp as she crushed them in her hands. She threw them at the wind and watched the bits of brown being whipped away by the afternoon wind.

"Who cares about the test, anyway," she said in a tight, grim whisper, tearing up another fistful of oak leaves. "Stupid test, stupid David, stupid cars. Who needs a license, anyway? Who needs a test like that?" It would only get harder, too, she realized, with the winter approaching and the streets turning slippery with the slush and snow. She had barely felt safe walking on the sidewalks in the winter—how could she possibly hope to drive then? It was hopeless, useless to even try. *I won't, I just won't ever take that test again!* Saeng told herself.

That resolved, she felt somewhat better. She turned away from the oak tree and was about to leave, when she suddenly noticed the bush next to it.

There was something very familiar about it. Some of its leaves had already blown off, but those that remained were still green. She picked a leaf and examined it. It was vaguely heart-shaped, with deeply serrated edges. Where had she seen this kind of leaf before? Saeng wondered. And why, among all these foreign maples and oak

117

leaves, did it seem so very familiar? She scrutinized the bush, but it was no help: If there had been any flowers on it, they had already fallen off.

Holding the leaf in her hand, Saeng left the park and started walking home.

Her pace was brisk and determined, and she had not planned to stop off anywhere But along the way, she found herself pausing involuntarily before a florist shop window. On display were bright bunches of cut flowers in tall glass vases—the splashes of red roses, white carnations, and yellow chrysanthemums a vivid contrast to the gray October afternoon. In the shadows behind them were several potted plants, none of which she could identify.

On an impulse, Saeng swung open the door and entered.

An elderly woman behind the counter looked up and smiled at her. "Yes? Can I help you?" she asked.

Saeng hesitated. Then she thrust out the heart-shaped green leaf in her hand and stammered, "Do—do you have this plant? I—I don't know its name."

The woman took the leaf and studied it with interest. "Why, yes," she said. "That looks like a rose of Sharon. We have several in the nursery out back."

She kept up a steady stream of conversation as she escorted Saeng through a side door into an open courtyard, where various saplings and shrubs stood. "Of course, it's not the best time for planting, but at least the ground hasn't frozen solid yet, and if you dig a deep enough hole and put in some good compost, it should do just fine. Hardy plants, these roses of Sharon. Pretty blossoms, too, in the fall. In fact—look, there's still a flower or two left on this shrub. Nice shade of pink, isn't it?"

Saeng looked at the single blossom left on the shrub. It looked small and washed out. The leaves on the shrub were of the same distinct serrated heart shape, but its flower looked—wrong, somehow.

"Is there—I mean, can it have another kind of flower?" Saeng asked. "Another color, maybe?"

"Well, it also comes in a pale purplish shade," the woman said helpfully. "And white, too."

"I think—I think it was a deep color," she offered, then shook her head. "I don't remember. It doesn't matter." Discouraged and feeling more than a little foolish, she started to back away.

"Wait," the florist said. "I think I know what you're looking for." A slow smile deepened the wrinkles in her face. "Come this way. It's in our greenhouse."

At the far side of the courtyard stood a shed, the like of which Saeng had never seen before. It was made entirely of glass and seemed to be bathed in a soft white light.

As she led the way there, the florist started talking again. "Lucky we just got through moving in some of our tropical plants," she said, "or the frost last weekend would have killed them off. Anything in there now you'd have to leave indoors until next summer, of course. Next to a big south-facing window or under some strong neon lamps. Even so, some of the plants won't survive the long cold winters here. Hothouse flowers, that's what they are. Not hardy, like those roses of Sharon I just showed you."

Only half listening, Saeng wished that there were a polite way she could excuse herself and leave. It was late and she was starting to get hungry. Still, she dutifully followed the other woman through the greenhouse door and walked in.

She gasped.

It was like walking into another world. A hot, moist world exploding with greenery. Huge flat leaves, delicate wisps of tendrils, ferns and fronds and vines of all shades and shapes grew in seemingly random profusion.

"Over there, in the corner, the hibiscus. Is that what you mean?" The florist pointed at a leafy potted plant by the corner.

There, in a shaft of the wan afternoon sunlight, was a single bloodred blossom, its five petals splayed back to reveal a long stamen tipped with yellow pollen. Saeng felt a shock of recognition so intense, it was almost visceral.

"*Saebba*," Saeng whispered.

A *saebba* hedge, tall and lush, had surrounded their garden, its lush green leaves dotted with vermilion flowers. And sometimes after a monsoon rain, a blossom or two would have blown into the well, so that when she drew up the well water, she would find a red blossom floating in the bucket.

Slowly, Saeng walked down the narrow aisle toward the hibiscus. Orchids, lanna bushes, oleanders, elephant ear begonias, and bougainvillaea vines surrounded her. Plants that she had not even realized she had known but had forgotten drew her back into her childhood world.

When she got to the hibiscus, she reached out and touched a petal gently. It felt smooth and cool, with a hint of velvet toward the center—just as she had known it would feel.

And beside it was yet another old friend, a small shrub with waxy leaves and dainty flowers with purplish petals and white centers. "Madagascar periwinkle," its tag announced. *How strange to see it in a pot,* Saeng thought. Back home it just grew wild, jutting out from the cracks in brick walls or between tiled roofs. There had been a patch of it by the little spirit house where she used to help her mother light the incense and candles to the spirit who guarded their home and their family. Sometimes she would casually pick a flower or two to leave on the offerings of fruit and rice left at the altar.

And that rich, sweet scent—that was familiar, too. Saeng scanned the greenery around her and found a tall, gangly plant with exquisite little white blossoms on it. "*Dok Malik,*" she said, savoring the feel of the word on her tongue, even as she silently noted the English name on its tag, "jasmine."

One of the blossoms had fallen off, and carefully Saeng picked it up and smelled it. She closed her eyes and breathed in, deeply. The familiar fragrance filled her lungs, and Saeng could almost feel the light strands of her grandmother's long gray hair, freshly washed, as she combed it out with the fine-toothed buffalo-horn comb. And when the sun had dried it, Saeng would help the gnarled old fingers knot the hair into a bun, then slip a *dok Malik* bud into it.

Saeng looked at the white bud in her hand now, small and fragile. Gently, she closed her palm around it and held it tight. That, at least, she could hold on to. But where was the fine-toothed comb? The hibiscus hedge? The well? Her gentle grandmother?

A wave of loss so deep and strong that it stung Saeng's eyes now swept over her. A blink, a channel switch, a boat ride in the night, and it was all gone. Irretrievably, irrevocably gone.

And in the warm moist shelter of the greenhouse, Saeng broke down and wept.

It was already dusk when Saeng reached home. The wind was

blowing harder, tearing off the last remnants of green in the chicory weeds that were growing out of the cracks in the sidewalk. As if oblivious to the cold, her mother was still out in the vegetable garden, digging up the last of the onions with a rusty trowel. She did not see Saeng until the girl had quietly knelt down next to her.

Her smile of welcome warmed Saeng. *"Ghup ma laio le?* You're back?" she said cheerfully. "Goodness, it's past five. What took you so long? How did it go? Did you—?" Then she noticed the potted plant that Saeng was holding, its leaves quivering in the wind.

Mrs. Panouvong uttered a small cry of surprise and delight. *"Dok faeng-noi!"* she said. "Where did you get it?"

"I bought it," Saeng answered, dreading her mother's next question.

"How much?"

For answer Saeng handed her mother some coins.

"That's all?" Mrs. Panouvong said, appalled. "Oh, but I forgot! You and the Lambert boy ate Bee-Maags...."

"No, we didn't, Mother," Saeng said.

"Then what else—?"

"Nothing else. I paid over nineteen dollars for it."

"You what?" Her mother stared at her incredulously. "But how could you? All the seeds for this vegetable garden didn't cost that much! You know how much we—" She paused, as she noticed the tearstains on her daughter's cheeks and her puffy eyes.

"What happened?" she asked, more gently.

"I—I failed the test," Saeng said.

For a long moment Mrs. Panouvong said nothing. Saeng did not dare to look her mother in the eye. Instead, she stared at the hibiscus plant and nervously tore off a leaf, shredding it to bits.

Her mother reached out and brushed the fragments of green off Saeng's hands. "It's a beautiful plant, this *dok faeng-noi*," she finally said. "I'm glad you got it."

"It's—it's not a real one," Saeng mumbled. "I mean, not like the kind we had at—at—" She found that she was still too shaky to say the words *at home*, lest she burst into tears again. "Not like the kind we had before," she said.

"I know," her mother said quietly. "I've seen this kind blooming along the lake. Its flowers aren't as pretty, but it's strong enough to

121

make it through the cold months here, this winter hibiscus. That's what matters."

She tipped the pot and deftly eased the ball of soil out, balancing the rest of the plant in her other hand. "Look how root-bound it is, poor thing," she said. "Let's plant it, right now."

She went over to the corner of the vegetable patch and started to dig a hole in the ground. The soil was cold and hard, and she had trouble thrusting the shovel into it. Wisps of her gray hair trailed out in the breeze, and her slight frown deepened the wrinkles around her eyes. There was a frail, wiry beauty to her that touched Saeng deeply.

"Here, let me help, Mother," she offered, getting up and taking the shovel away from her.

Mrs. Panouvong made no resistance. "I'll bring in the hot peppers and bitter melons, then, and start dinner. How would you like an omelet with slices of the bitter melon?"

"I'd love it," Saeng said.

Left alone in the garden, Saeng dug out a hole and carefully lowered the "winter hibiscus" into it. She could hear the sounds of cooking from the kitchen now, the beating of the eggs against a bowl, the sizzle of hot oil in the pan. The pungent smell of bitter melon wafted out, and Saeng's mouth watered. It was a cultivated taste, she had discovered—none of her classmates or friends, not even Mrs. Lambert, liked it—this sharp, bitter melon that left a golden aftertaste on the tongue. But she had grown up eating it and, she admitted to herself, much preferred it to a Big Mac.

The "winter hibiscus" was in the ground now, and Saeng tamped down the soil around it. Overhead, a flock of Canada geese flew by, their faint honks clear and—yes—familiar to Saeng now. Almost reluctantly, she realized that many of the things that she had thought of as strange before had become, through the quiet repetition of season upon season, almost familiar to her now. Like the geese. She lifted her head and watched as their distinctive V was etched against the evening sky, slowly fading into the distance.

When they come back, Saeng vowed silently to herself, in the spring, when the snows melt and the geese return and this hibiscus is budding, then I will take that test again.

The Negro Speaks of Rivers

by Langston Hughes

I've known rivers:
I've known rivers ancient as the world and older than the
   flow of human blood in human veins.

My soul has grown deep like the rivers.

I bathed in the Euphrates when dawns were young.
I built my hut near the Congo and it lulled me to sleep.
I looked upon the Nile and raised the pyramids above it.
I heard the singing of the Mississippi when Abe Lincoln
   went down to New Orleans, and I've seen its muddy
   bosom turn all golden in the sunset.

I've known rivers:
Ancient, dusky rivers.

My soul has grown deep like the rivers.

Borders

by Thomas King

*When the narrator and his mother leave the reser-
vation in Canada to visit his older sister, it seems like a
simple trip. But the mother's strong sense of who she is
leads to an international incident—and lessons in
identity for everyone.*

When I was 12, maybe 13, my mother announced that we were going to go to Salt Lake City to visit my sister who had left the reserve, moved across the line, and found a job. Laetitia had not left home with my mother's blessing, but over time my mother had come to be proud of the fact that Laetitia had done all of this on her own.

"She did real good," my mother would say.

Then there were the fine points to Laetitia's going. She had not, as my mother liked to tell Mrs. Manyfingers, gone floating after some man like a balloon on a string. She hadn't snuck out of the house, either, and gone to Vancouver or Edmonton or Toronto to chase rainbows down alleys. And she hadn't been pregnant.

"She did real good."

I was seven or eight when Laetitia left home. She was 17. Our father was from Rocky Boy on the American side.

"Dad's American," Laetitia told my mother, "so I can go and come as I please."

"Send us a postcard."

Laetitia packed her things, and we headed for the border. Just outside of Milk River, Laetitia told us to watch for the water tower.

"Over the next rise. It's the first thing you see."

"We got a water tower on the reserve," my mother said. "There's a big one in Lethbridge, too."

"You'll be able to see the tops of the flagpoles, too. That's where the border is."

When we got to Coutts, my mother stopped at the convenience store and bought her and Laetitia a cup of coffee. I got an Orange Crush.

"This is real lousy coffee."

"You're just angry because I want to see the world."

"It's the water. From here on down, they got lousy water."

"I can catch the bus from Sweetgrass. You don't have to lift a finger."

"You're going to have to buy your water in bottles if you want good coffee."

There was an old wooden building about a block away, with a tall sign in the yard that said "Museum." Most of the roof had been blown away. Mom told me to go and see when the place was open. There were boards over the windows and doors. You could tell that the place was closed, and I told Mom so, but she said to go and check anyway. Mom and Laetitia stayed by the car. Neither one of them moved. I sat down on the steps of the museum and watched them, and I don't know that they ever said anything to each other. Finally, Laetitia got her bag out of the trunk and gave Mom a hug.

I wandered back to the car. The wind had come up, and it blew Laetitia's hair across her face. Mom reached out and pulled the strands out of Laetitia's eyes, and Laetitia let her.

"You can still see the mountain from here," my mother told Laetitia in Blackfoot.

"Lots of mountains in Salt Lake," Laetitia told her in English.

"The place is closed," I said. "Just like I told you."

Laetitia tucked her hair into her jacket and dragged her bag down the road to the brick building with the American flag flapping on a pole. When she got to where the guards were waiting, she turned,

125

put the bag down, and waved to us. We waved back. Then my mother turned the car around, and we came home.

We got postcards from Laetitia regular, and, if she wasn't spreading jelly on the truth, she was happy. She found a good job and rented an apartment with a pool.

"And she can't even swim," my mother told Mrs. Manyfingers.

Most of the postcards said we should come down and see the city, but whenever I mentioned this, my mother would stiffen up.

So I was surprised when she bought two new tires for the car and put on her blue dress with the green and yellow flowers. I had to dress up, too, for my mother did not want us crossing the border looking like Americans. We made sandwiches and put them in a big box with pop and potato chips and some apples and bananas and a big jar of water.

"But we can stop at one of those restaurants, too, right?"

"We maybe should take some blankets in case you get sleepy."

"But we can stop at one of those restaurants, too, right?"

The border was actually two towns, though neither one was big enough to amount to anything. Coutts was on the Canadian side and consisted of the convenience store and gas station, the museum that was closed and boarded up, and a motel. Sweetgrass was on the American side, but all you could see was an overpass that arched across the highway and disappeared into the prairies. Just hearing the names of these towns, you would expect that Sweetgrass, which is a nice name and sounds like it is related to other places such as Medicine Hat and Moose Jaw and Kicking Horse Pass, would be on the Canadian side, and that Coutts, which sounds abrupt and rude, would be on the American side. But this was not the case.

Between the two borders was a duty-free shop where you could buy cigarettes and liquor and flags. Stuff like that.

We left the reserve in the morning and drove until we got to Coutts.

"Last time we stopped here," my mother said, "you had an Orange Crush. You remember that?"

"Sure," I said. "That was when Laetitia took off."

"You want another Orange Crush?"

"That means we're not going to stop at a restaurant, right?"

My mother got a coffee at the convenience store, and we stood around and watched the prairies move in the sunlight. Then we

126

climbed back in the car. My mother straightened the dress across her thighs, leaned against the wheel, and drove all the way to the border in first gear, slowly, as if she were trying to see through a bad storm or riding high on black ice.

The border guard was an old guy. As he walked to the car, he swayed from side to side, his feet set wide apart, the holster on his hip pitching up and down. He leaned into the window, looked into the back seat, and looked at my mother and me.

"Morning, ma'am."

"Good morning."

"Where you heading?"

"Salt Lake City."

"Purpose of your visit?"

"Visit my daughter."

"Citizenship?"

"Blackfoot," my mother told him.

"Ma'am?"

"Blackfoot," my mother repeated.

"Canadian?"

"Blackfoot."

It would have been easier if my mother had just said "Canadian" and been done with it, but I could see she wasn't going to do that. The guard wasn't angry or anything. He smiled and looked towards the building. Then he turned back and nodded.

"Morning, ma'am."

"Good morning."

"Any firearms or tobacco?"

"No."

"Citizenship?"

"Blackfoot."

He told us to sit in the car and wait, and we did. In about five minutes, another guard came out with the first man. They were talking as they came, both men swaying back and forth like two cowboys headed for a bar or a gunfight.

"Morning, ma'am."

"Good morning."

"Cecil tells me you and the boy are Blackfoot."

"That's right."

"Now, I know that we got Blackfeet on the American side and the Canadians got Blackfeet on their side. Just so we can keep our records straight, what side do you come from?"

I knew exactly what my mother was going to say, and I could have told them if they had asked me.

"Canadian side or American side?" asked the guard.

"Blackfoot side," she said.

It didn't take them long to lose their sense of humor, I can tell you that. The one guard stopped smiling altogether and told us to park our car at the side of the building and come in.

We sat on a wood bench for about an hour before anyone came over to talk to us. This time it was a woman. She had a gun, too.

"Hi," she said. "I'm Inspector Pratt. I understand there is a little misunderstanding."

"I'm going to visit my daughter in Salt Lake City," my mother told her. "We don't have any guns or beer."

"It's a legal technicality, that's all."

"My daughter's Blackfoot, too."

The woman opened a briefcase and took out a couple of forms and began to write on one of them. "Everyone who crosses our border has to declare their citizenship. Even Americans. It helps us keep track of the visitors we get from the various countries."

She went on like that for maybe fifteen minutes, and a lot of the stuff she told us was interesting.

"I can understand how you feel about having to tell us your citizenship, and here's what I'll do. You tell me, and I won't put it down on the form. No one will know but you and me."

Her gun was silver. There were several chips in the wood handle and the name "Stella" was scratched into the metal butt.

We were in the border office for about four hours, and we talked to almost everyone there. One of the men bought me a Coke. My mother brought a couple of sandwiches in from the car. I offered part of mine to Stella, but she said she wasn't hungry.

I told Stella that we were Blackfoot and Canadian, but she said that that didn't count because I was a minor. In the end, she told us that if my mother didn't declare her citizenship, we would have to go back to where we came from. My mother stood up and thanked Stella for her time. Then we got back in the car and drove to the Canadian border, which was only about a hundred yards away.

I was disappointed. I hadn't seen Laetitia for a long time, and I had never been to Salt Lake City. When she was still at home, Laetitia would go on and on about Salt Lake City. She had never been there, but her boyfriend Lester Tallbull had spent a year in Salt Lake at a technical school.

"It's a great place," Lester would say. "Nothing but blondes in the whole state."

Whenever he said that, Laetitia would slug him on his shoulder hard enough to make him flinch. He had some brochures on Salt Lake and some maps, and every so often the two of them would spread them out on the table.

"That's the temple. It's right downtown. You got to have a pass to get in."

"Charlotte says anyone can go in and look around."

"When was Charlotte in Salt Lake? Just when the hell was Charlotte in Salt Lake?"

"Last year."

"This is Liberty Park. It's got a zoo. There's good skiing in the mountains."

"Got all the skiing we can use," my mother would say. "People come from all over the world to ski at Banff. Cardston's got a temple, if you like those kinds of things."

"Oh, this one is real big," Lester would say. "They got armed guards and everything."

"Not what Charlotte says."

"What does she know?"

Lester and Laetitia broke up, but I guess the idea of Salt Lake stuck in her mind.

The Canadian border guard was a young woman, and she seemed happy to see us. "Hi," she said. "You folks sure have a great day for a trip. Where are you coming from?"

"Standoff."

"Is that in Montana?"

"No."

"Where are you going?"

"Standoff."

The woman's name was Carol and I don't guess she was any older than Laetitia. "Wow, you both Canadians?"

"Blackfoot."

"Really? I have a friend I went to school with who is Blackfoot. Do you know Mike Harley?"

"No."

"He went to school in Lethbridge, but he's really from Browning."

It was a nice conversation and there were no cars behind us, so there was no rush.

"You're not bringing any liquor back, are you?"

"No."

"Any cigarettes or plants or stuff like that?"

"No."

"Citizenship?"

"Blackfoot."

"I know," said the woman, "and I'd be proud of being Blackfoot if I were Blackfoot. But you have to be American or Canadian."

When Laetitia and Lester broke up, Lester took his brochures and maps with him, so Laetitia wrote to someone in Salt Lake City, and, about a month later, she got a big envelope of stuff. We sat at the table and opened up all the brochures, and Laetitia read each one out loud.

"Salt Lake City is the gateway to some of the world's most magnificent skiing.

"Salt Lake City is the home of one of the newest professional basketball franchises, the Utah Jazz.

"The Great Salt Lake is one of the natural wonders of the world."

It was kind of exciting seeing all those color brochures on the table and listening to Laetitia read all about how Salt Lake City was one of the best places in the entire world.

"That Salt Lake City place sounds too good to be true," my mother told her.

"It has everything."

"We got everything right here."

"It's boring here."

"People in Salt Lake City are probably sending away for brochures of Calgary and Lethbridge and Pincher Creek right now."

In the end, my mother would say that maybe Laetitia should go to Salt Lake City, and Laetitia would say that maybe she would.

We parked the car to the side of the building and Carol led us into a small room on the second floor. I found a comfortable spot on the couch and flipped through some back issues of *Saturday Night* and *Alberta Report*.

When I woke up, my mother was just coming out of another office. She didn't say a word to me. I followed her down the stairs and out to the car. I thought we were going home, but she turned the car around and drove back towards the American border, which made me think we were going to visit Laetitia in Salt Lake City after all. Instead she pulled into the parking lot of the duty-free store and stopped.

"We going to see Laetitia?"

"No."

"We going home?"

Pride is a good thing to have, you know. Laetitia had a lot of pride, and so did my mother. I figured that someday, I'd have it, too.

"So where are we going?"

Most of that day, we wandered around the duty-free store, which wasn't very large. The manager had a name tag with a tiny American flag on one side and a tiny Canadian flag on the other. His name was Mel. Towards evening, he began suggesting that we should be on our way. I told him we had nowhere to go, that neither the Americans nor the Canadians would let us in. He laughed at that and told us that we should buy something or leave.

The car was not very comfortable, but we did have all that food and it was April, so even if it did snow as it sometimes does on the prairies, we wouldn't freeze. The next morning my mother drove to the American border.

It was a different guard this time, but the questions were the same. We didn't spend as much time in the office as we had the day before. By noon, we were back at the Canadian border. By two we were back in the duty-free-shop parking lot.

The second night in the car was not as much fun as the first, but my mother seemed in good spirits, and, all in all, it was as much an adventure as an inconvenience. There wasn't much food left and that was a problem, but we had lots of water as there was a faucet at the side of the duty-free shop.

One Sunday, Laetitia and I were watching television. Mom was over at Mrs. Manyfingers's. Right in the middle of the program, Laetitia turned off the set and said she was going to Salt Lake City, that life around here was too boring. I had wanted to see the rest of the program and really didn't care if Laetitia went to Salt Lake City or not. When Mom got home, I told her what Laetitia had said.

What surprised me was how angry Laetitia got when she found out that I had told Mom.

"You got a big mouth."

"That's what you said."

"What I said is none of your business."

"I didn't say anything."

"Well, I'm going for sure, now."

That weekend, Laetitia packed her bags, and we drove her to the border.

Mel turned out to be friendly. When he closed up for the night and found us still parked in the lot, he came over and asked us if our car was broken down or something. My mother thanked him for his concern and told him that we were fine, that things would get straightened out in the morning.

"You're kidding," said Mel. "You'd think they could handle the simple things."

"We got some apples and a banana," I said, "but we're all out of ham sandwiches."

"You know, you read about these things, but you just don't believe it. You just don't believe it."

"Hamburgers would be even better because they got more stuff for energy."

My mother slept in the back seat. I slept in the front because I was smaller and could lie under the steering wheel. Late that night, I heard my mother open the car door. I found her sitting on her blanket leaning against the bumper of the car.

"You see all those stars," she said. "When I was a little girl, my grandmother used to take me and my sisters out on the prairies and tell us stories about all the stars."

132

"Do you think Mel is going to bring us any hamburgers?"

"Every one of those stars has a story. You see that bunch of stars over there that look like a fish?"

"He didn't say no."

"Coyote went fishing, one day. That's how it all started." We sat out under the stars that night, and my mother told me all sorts of stories. She was serious about it, too. She'd tell them slow, repeating parts as she went, as if she expected me to remember each one.

Early the next morning, the television vans began to arrive, and guys in suits and women in dresses came trotting over to us, dragging microphones and cameras and lights behind them. One of the vans had a table set up with orange juice and sandwiches and fruit. It was for the crew, but when I told them we hadn't eaten for a while, a really skinny blonde woman told us we could eat as much as we wanted.

They mostly talked to my mother. Every so often one of the reporters would come over and ask me questions about how it felt to be an Indian without a country. I told them we had a nice house on the reserve and that my cousins had a couple of horses we rode when we went fishing. Some of the television people went over to the American border, and then they went to the Canadian border.

Around noon, a good-looking guy in a dark blue suit and an orange tie with little ducks on it drove up in a fancy car. He talked to my mother for a while, and after they were done talking, my mother called me over, and we got into our car. Just as my mother started the engine, Mel came over and gave us a bag of peanut brittle and told us that justice was a damn hard thing to get, but that we shouldn't give up.

I would have preferred lemon drops, but it was nice of Mel anyway.

"Where are we going now?"

"Going to visit Laetitia."

The guard who came out to our car was all smiles. The television lights were so bright they hurt my eyes, and, if you tried to look through the windshield in certain directions, you couldn't see a thing.

"Morning, ma'am."

"Good morning."

"Where you heading?"

"Salt Lake City."

"Purpose of your visit?"

"Visit my daughter."

"Any tobacco, liquor, or firearms?"

"Don't smoke."

"Any plants or fruit?"

"Not any more."

"Citizenship?"

"Blackfoot."

The guard rocked back on his heels and jammed his thumbs into his gun belt. "Thank you," he said, his fingers patting the butt of the revolver. "Have a pleasant trip."

My mother rolled the car forward, and the television people had to scramble out of the way. They ran alongside the car as we pulled away from the border, and, when they couldn't run any farther, they stood in the middle of the highway and waved and waved and waved.

We got to Salt Lake City the next day. Laetitia was happy to see us, and, that first night, she took us out to a restaurant that made really good soups. The list of pies took up a whole page. I had cherry. Mom had chocolate. Laetitia said that she saw us on television the night before and, during the meal, she had us tell her the story over and over again.

Laetitia took us everywhere. We went to a fancy ski resort. We went to the temple. We got to go shopping in a couple of large malls, but they weren't as large as the one in Edmonton, and Mom said so.

After a week or so, I got bored and wasn't at all sad when my mother said we should be heading back home. Laetitia wanted us to stay longer, but Mom said no, that she had things to do back home and that, next time, Laetitia should come up and visit. Laetitia said she was thinking about moving back, and Mom told her to do as she pleased, and Laetitia said that she would.

On the way home, we stopped at the duty-free shop, and my mother gave Mel a green hat that said "Salt Lake" across the front. Mel was a funny guy. He took the hat and blew his nose and told my mother that she was an inspiration to us all. He gave us some more peanut brittle and came out into the parking lot and waved at us all the way to the Canadian border.

It was almost evening when we left Coutts. I watched the border through the rear window until all you could see were the tops of the flagpoles and the blue water tower, and then they rolled over a hill and disappeared.

Foreign Student

by Barbara B. Robinson

In September she appeared
    row three, seat seven,
    heavy pleated skirt,
    plastic purse, tidy notepad,
there she sat,
silent,
straight from Tai Pei,
and she bowed
when I entered the room.
A model student
I noticed,
    though she walked
    alone through the halls,
every assignment neat,
on time, complete,
and she'd listen
when I talked.

But now it's May
and Si Lan
is called Lani.
She strides in
with Noriyo and Lynne
and Natavidad.
She wears slacks.
Her gear is crammed
into a macramé
shoulder sack.
And she chatters with Pete
during class
and I'm glad.

Godmother

by Sharon Bell Mathis

It isn't easy for Willa to learn to understand her godmother, in all her complexity. But when she does, she learns a lot about herself as well.

Although Willa had never met her godmother, she recognized the woman immediately. "Your Aunt Beverly's got a headful of soft white hair, the plumpest cutest face, and the deepest dimples in Washington, D.C.," her mother had said, laughing. "Bev had a few strands of gray in her hair when we weren't but two little girls in Baltimore. We used to call her 'old lady' for fun. Our families lived side by side, and she was my best double-Dutch partner. Bev was fat— but she could jump in and out of a rope faster than anybody else on the block."

Now Aunt Beverly, looking much older than the pictures she regularly sent to Willa, was lumbering across the black-and-white marble floors of Union Station.

Willa bolted up from the worn suitcase she was sitting on and met the woman halfway. "Hi, Aunt Beverly," Willa said, and hugged the short heavyset woman, her face framed by two thick, silver-colored braids pinned close to her head.

Aunt Beverly, dressed in an old-fashioned dark green linen suit, with matching dark green linen pumps, stepped back and stared at Willa. "My," she said, "I didn't realize you had grown so."

"I'm 14, Aunt Beverly," Willa said, hugging the woman again.

"Fourteen—and you're so tall."

"Uh-huh," Willa fussed, grabbing her suitcase. "And I'm trying not to think of how much taller I'll be tomorrow morning!"

"That valise has seen a better day," Aunt Beverly said, irritated. "We'll have to get you another."

"This is Mama's suitcase—"

"We'll have to get you another."

"I don't need a new suitcase, Aunt Beverly. This one is fine. I take it whenever I spend the night somewhere. I don't need a new one."

"'Godmother,'" Aunt Beverly said. "I'm your godmother, and that is what you will call me." There wasn't even a hint of a smile on her face.

"Mama said to call you 'Aunt Beverly.' I always call you 'Aunt Beverly,'" Willa said, feeling the first nervous tic in her stomach, knowing that if she ever said "Aunt Beverly" again, there would be trouble. Willa watched silently as a Union Station redcap placed her scratched suitcase in the trunk of a taxicab. In the cab, Willa sat as far away from Godmother as she could.

"No more 'Aunt Beverly,' and I can't imagine why Angela wouldn't have you call me 'Godmother' from the beginning. I am not your aunt. Say 'Godmother,' I don't think it's very difficult to pronounce."

"Godmother," Willa managed, leaning away more.

Godmother moved close to Willa and hugged the quiet girl tightly. "Look at me," she said to Willa. Willa did. She saw that Godmother's dimples were the deepest she had ever seen.

"Doesn't saying 'Godmother' sound better?"

Willa didn't answer.

"You're my godchild," Godmother continued. "You're like my own child—you are my child. In fact, your father noticed me before he ever noticed your mother. I don't suppose Angela mentioned that. I was really quite surprised when they married. I was away in college, you know. Your mother and I graduated high school together, but she and Thomas fell in love and married and had all those babies. I went on to college and became a teacher."

All those babies!

"Life was hard, and I had to struggle. I was on my own—I know Angela had to tell you that. My mother died when I was young. I had it hard, but it made me strong. I learned early what I was made of."

My father didn't want you. He loved my mother!

"I thank God for everything that ever happened to me because I learned lessons I could never have learned in any other way."

Well, I'm glad you learned them. Big deal.

"Your mother, Angela, had both her mother and her father and her sisters and her brothers. I didn't have any of that. I had my daddy, and that was all." Godmother leaned forward and stared at Willa. "Honey," she asked, "is that lipstick you're wearing—at 14?"

"It's just lip gloss."

"'Godmother.'"

"Godmother, it's just lip gloss."

"You have features just like your mother—the exact same lips, a little full. We—the kids, you know—would call her 'Libba Lips.' Oh, I remember that."

"That was mean, Godmother," Willa said with as much evil in her voice as she could summon.

"It wasn't mean—and Angela didn't mind."

"She did mind. Mama told me when people called her 'Libba Lips,' it meant that they were ignorant and stupid to call her names and hurt her." Willa's mother had never said such a thing to Willa—but Godmother didn't know that. "My mother knows there's nothing wrong with her lips! She has beautiful lips!"

"If she didn't think anything was wrong with her lips—why was she hurt?" Godmother asked, smiling.

You're the meanest godmother on earth.

"But why are we talking about Angela's lips? There are so many other things to talk about. Angela sent your report card to me. Straight A's. She was very proud. So was I."

"Mama's very smart, too," Willa said, quickly adding, "and she's kind to people. Everybody loves my mother. My brother and my sisters are smart, too. My brother was on television because he designed and built a model house—and he can sing and play a piano. Mama's never mean to people." *Like you!*

That cab felt stuffy to Willa, her cornrowed braids felt prickly at her neck, her body shiny with sweat, her stomach uneasy. Willa wanted to go back home.

"Yes, your mother's smart, but she didn't do anything with it—just got married and had those babies. Of course, she was very lucky to have children—and smart children at that. She has everything. I just have you."

You don't have me.

"I have many lovely activities planned for you this summer. I told Angela I don't want you to leave until Labor Day. I asked if you could stay the whole summer, and she agreed. That sweet letter you sent to me a few weeks ago mentioned that you would be happy to spend the summer with me."

I didn't know you were mean!

"We're going to have a wonderful summer. My child is here at last."

Godmother was still talking about the fun they would have when the taxi pulled up in front of a large red brick house with a vividly blooming flower garden—in a circular-patterned bed, edged with weathered railroad ties. Willa thought the house was beautiful, like a picture in a magazine.

The cab driver set Willa's suitcase on the front porch, took the money Godmother held out to him, and walked rapidly down the wide brick steps.

Willa wanted to run down the steps behind him, climb back into the cab, get on another train, and go back home to her mother— Angela. Angela, who was so proud of her lifelong friend Beverly who had become a teacher and who lived in such a lovely house with such a lovely flower garden on Kalmia Road. Angela, a poet and an artist, but who hadn't done anything except "get married and have all those babies." Willa, Deanna, Marlena, her brother Tommy, and her deceased father, Thomas, all reduced to zero by a fat woman who had once called her mother "Libba Lips."

"Mama can draw flowers that look more real than these," Willa said without a second glance at the brilliant, profuse colors.

"Now, that she could do," Godmother said. "She was drawing all the time. Drawing, reading poems, writing poems—and sewing. That was Angela. I can see her now—in those big plaits she used to wear, ribbons tied on and all. My mother was dead, and there was nobody to put ribbons in my hair. Certainly not my father—although he did the best he could. My hair just fell loose most of the time. I didn't know what to do with it myself. Thank God it was curly."

Just then, a tall girl—even taller than Willa—ran across the heavily treelined street and up onto the porch just as Godmother opened the door to the house. "Hi, Ms. Beverly," she said and reached for Willa's arm. "I'm Debby. I live right across the street in that house," she said, pointing to what looked like a mansion to Willa. Debby put her arms around Willa. "I've been counting the days until you got here," she said. "We're the only teenagers on this street!"

Willa looked at Debby's warm dark face, framed by closely cropped hair decorated with a single clip of African trade beads, and she smiled a real smile. "Hi," Willa said.

"Debby," Godmother said impatiently, "Willa's just arrived, and she's tired and wants to rest. You run back home now. We'll see you later."

"Why does she have to go, Godmother? I'm not tired."

"I'll be back!" Debby yelled, already running back across the street. It was then that Willa noticed the scalloped edge on the bottom of the girl's denim shorts; white eyelet lace was showing through the scalloped edges. Willa wanted a pair of shorts exactly like them.

Godmother's house was totally white throughout. The furniture was upholstered in a white silk brocade fabric. There was a huge white baby grand piano—just like Duke Ellington's. Willa stopped breathing when she saw it. If only her brother, Tommy, could have a chance to play it. If only her brother could *see* it!

There were tiny figurines of white men and women—dressed like those in the movie *Gone With the Wind*—all over the mantel. In what Godmother called a curio cabinet, there were glass shelves filled with miniature birds in birds' nests, and miniature white children—boys in fancy pantaloons and girls in pale smocked dresses. There were lead crystal cups and saucers and dishes of every sort. Godmother told Willa the names of each one of the formal, smiling youngsters. "These are my children," she said. Godmother touched one ballerina dressed in a delicately shaded costume, balanced on one toe, her arms outstretched. "This one is my dancer," she announced with obvious pride.

Willa looked around the large living room and saw more white people, once again dressed in elaborate costumes, in ornate, heavy gold wooden frames. Willa thought of her own home with framed posters of the Dance Theatre of Harlem—signed by six of the dancers, a Romare Bearden print commemorating Brown *vs.* the Board of Education, Tom Feelings's *Bed-Stuy on a Saturday Afternoon*, prints of Charles White's muscular African Americans, and the photographs of Gordon Parks, Van der Zee, Roland Freeman, and Moneta Sleet.

Willa thought of the bedroom she shared with her sisters Marlena and Deanna, where there was a framed book jacket of John Steptoe's *Mufaro's Beautiful Daughters,* signed by the author/illustrator. Willa's mother had had to stand in line for two hours, heart disease and all, to have the book jacket signed by the young author and illustrator of children's books. It had been Angela's Christmas present to her daughters. Willa's brother, Tommy, had received an autographed book, *Fallen Angels,* by Walter Dean Myers. Tommy's room was decorated with pictures of Herbie Hancock and Van Cliburn.

But now Willa was standing in a room filled with "expensive" figurines, John Steptoe was dead, and a beloved signed photograph of Herbie Hancock seated at a piano, lovingly placed atop a plain maple bureau, seemed a hundred million miles away.

"Is it all right if I take my suitcase to my room now?" Willa asked, hoping to get away by herself for a moment. Of course, it would be better if Debby came back over right now, this minute, today.

"Let me show you where your room is," Godmother answered, "and tell you a bit about where to find a few things you may need."

When Willa saw her room, she loved it immediately. It was decorated in several shades of pale lavender. The bedspread was an exact match for the wallpaper—tiny sprays of purple flowers caught up with lovely white ribbons and bows. The window shades matched the bedspread and wallpaper! The curtains were edged in white organdy. The furniture was mahogany—dark and shiny. But the best thing of all was the bed—with four posts almost to the ceiling. Stretched across the top, anchored by the four posts, was a canopy of the same fabric, more of the tiny flowers.

"Your mother said you loved purple, so I had the room done over for you."

Willa couldn't believe this beautiful room was all hers. If only her sisters could see it!

"Personally, it's a bit too fussy for me. I'd never be able to sleep in a room this busy-looking."

Willa was still staring at the fancy room.

"The decorators assured me that you'd be pleased."

"I love it!"

"Good," Godmother said, and began to open dresser drawers, pointing out slips and bras and panties and socks and stockings. In the closet were three new dresses, some skirts, and a few blouses. "Your mother sent your sizes, as I asked her to do. I wasn't sure if Angela had enough money to buy your summer clothes, and I didn't want you to look any different from the other girls around here. Shoes we'll buy tomorrow. A pair for dress-up, and some sandals. We'll get a bathing suit as well. Debby has a lovely pool in her yard."

A *pool!*

"I know your mother makes most of your clothes."

That was true, but Willa was mighty glad to see all this new stuff. Besides that, Marlena and Deanna—almost as tall as she was—could certainly share all this bounty.

There was even a purplish plaid dress with the back out.

"Debby picked that one," Godmother said, sounding annoyed. "It's a bit too much, I think. Rather naked. You certainly can't wear it to church."

"Is there a Catholic church near here?"

"I wouldn't know. You'll go to church with me. Episcopalian, just like a Catholic church. You'll feel right at home."

Episcopalian?

"Take a bath and take a nap, child. When you get up, dinner will be ready, and we'll have an opportunity to talk to one another."

"Can I call my mother?"

"'*May* I call my mother?'"

"May I call my mother? Please."

"Of course."

While Willa was dialing the telephone, she heard Godmother walking quickly down the steps. As soon as Willa heard her mother's voice on the telephone, she also heard Godmother pick up the downstairs extension.

"Hi, Ma," Willa said, and tried to keep her voice light. "Godmother's on the phone, too, and we just wanted to let you know that I got here safely."

"That's great, sweetheart! Have a good time, and don't worry about anything. She's my worrier, Bev. I told you that." Willa wanted to go through the telephone wires and get back to her mother, back to her home, back to her family—leave the purple-flowered room behind.

"I don't know why she would be worried. I was at that train station an hour ahead of time." Godmother sounded angry, and Willa didn't know why. "I was going to call you myself later, but Willa wanted to do it now. She's been talking about you since the moment she arrived. She really is a 'Mama's girl.'"

"She loves you, too, Bev," Willa heard her mother say quietly. "She's been looking forward to visiting you for a long time now."

"Well, I'm only the godmother—but she's mine while she's here. She's safe, and she has a lovely room to sleep in and good food to eat, and as you know, I've loved her since the day she was born."

"I know that, Bev."

"As much as you love her."

"Bev—"

"So I hope she doesn't think she's going to call you night and day and every morning."

"She knows what to do, Bev."

"I remember the night she was born—a snowy night. Didn't it snow, Ange?"

"Yes, it did, Bev."

"It was snowing here and in Baltimore. That's why I couldn't get to the hospital, couldn't get a train out. God knows, I tried. When Tom called and told me you were ready to deliver, I just sat at the window looking out at the falling snow and praying. I never prayed so hard before, praying the baby would be a girl and praying that she would be all right. I prayed so hard."

"I know you did, Bev."

"You had promised me that I'd be the godmother to your first baby. I said to God: 'God, this one is mine—don't let anything happen to this child, and please, let it be a little girl.' And God did just that. He gave me that little baby girl."

"Yes, He did, Bev."

"I got there as soon as I could after that, didn't I?"

143

"Yes, you did."

"I was a college student. I didn't have much money, but I came to you anyway."

"Yes, you did."

Willa listened to Godmother talking about when she had first held Willa and how tightly Willa had held Godmother's finger. Finally, Willa spoke again. "See you, Mama," she said quietly into the telephone, and put the receiver down—disconnecting from her mother's quiet voice.

Willa rebraided her two long cornrows, folded back the beautiful bedspread and matching sheets, and flopped diagonally across the bed—her long feet hanging over. Willa listened to Godmother's voice, listened to her godmother mentioning all of the gifts she had sent to Willa over the years. "And now that little baby girl is here with her godmother—spending the summer, and I thank you, Ange." Willa listened until somehow she fell asleep.

She tried to make herself dream about home. It didn't work. Willa dreamed she was growing taller.

At dinner, Willa noticed that Godmother's speech seemed more pronounced, more deliberate, slower. Her voice became even more so throughout the evening, as Godmother sipped discolored milk from a crystal cocktail glass. "This is my brandy," she said.

"I didn't know you could drink brandy while you're a diabetic and have to give yourself insulin shots in your stomach."

"Don't be stupid, Willa!"

"Stupid?"

"Yes. I said brandy, not whiskey. Brandy. B-R-A-N-D-Y!"

"I didn't know you—"

"There's a lot you don't know, judging from the letters you write. Capital letters everywhere, and run-on sentences to boot. Your sentences stretch out and out, not a comma or a semicolon to be seen. In your two-page letters, you generally have one period, my dear. One period. Period!"

Willa felt her heart stop. In all of Godmother's return letters, she had never once mentioned commas, periods, and colons. And now here was Godmother laughing at letters Willa had written so very long ago. Making fun of them!

"Brandy is nothing but wine. My doctor—the only decent one I have—tells me that brandy is good for me. You don't know what's good for me. Unless I missed something in these years since you were born, you're not a doctor."

Willa tried to finish her dinner, but she couldn't.

"Your mother drinks."

"She does not."

"Well, she should."

Willa got up from the table and went back upstairs to her room and stood there in the near dark. The bright purple flowers looked black, the white organdy grayish.

"I could use some help down here in the kitchen with these dishes," Godmother called up the steps, her words slurred and cold. "If you come back down, I'd certainly appreciate it."

Willa went back down and entered the kitchen.

"Now, that's better," Godmother said, "and don't worry about my drinking brandy. I know more about diabetes than you'll ever know— and I *do* hope you *never* know. I'm happy you're young and healthy. When I was 14, I was healthy, too. When your mother was 14, she was healthy as well. Do you think she had a bad heart then? Well, I'm here to tell you that she certainly did not!"

While Willa was putting dishes into the dishwasher, Debby came over and Godmother let her stay. Godmother went to bed and the two girls giggled and laughed over many things. The purple flowers were bright again. Willa asked Debby where she had bought the denim shorts with the scalloped edges and white eyelet lace. Willa said she hoped they weren't expensive. "I've got 50 dollars, but it has to last me all summer."

"Heck," Debby said, "I made these. I can make them for you for about six dollars—including the zipper if we can get the material on sale."

"You *made* those shorts?"

"Yep—and anything else you see me wear."

"You gotta be kidding, kiddo!"

"I started sewing when I was seven."

Willa was amazed. "Seven?"

"Yep! My mom and I were at a thrift store—she was taking her clothes to them so that the store can make some money—and I saw this old beat-up sewing machine and started hollering and screaming so that she would get frustrated and buy it for me. I was right. She bought it to shut me up. My mother learned to sew on that machine, trying to teach me how to sew. She kept saying, well, I'm certainly not going to buy a new one for you to play with. Both of us learned to sew, and then she got bored and stopped and I kept on going. The only thing better than sewing is kissing Denzel Washington."

"Juicy kiss," Willa said, squealing.

"A down-home, grits-cooking kiss."

"Do you get a chance to kiss anybody?" Willa asked.

"No," Debby said, suddenly serious. "Do you?"

"Nope!"

The two girls laughed harder about that than anything they had laughed at before. "Maybe one day," Willa said.

"Yep!"

"And please, God, let it be Denzel Washington," the two girls said together.

"Guess what, Debby?"

"What?"

"My mother sews all the time, and I never even look at the machine!"

"Guess what, Willa?"

"What?"

"You're going to make your own shorts."

Willa stopped giggling then and begged Debby to reconsider. "I can't do it, I can't sew anything. I mean *nuthin'!*"

Debby insisted. "If you want them, you're gonna make them."

If Willa hadn't loved the scalloped shorts so much, she would have given up the idea right there and then. She knew Debby meant what she had said.

A short time later, Willa walked across the street with Debby, who was going home. It was 10 o'clock at night. "I'm glad you exist," Willa said. "Godmother's kind of mean."

"She just gets real particular when she's drinking, that's all. She's so much fun—and real sweet to everybody. She talks about you all the time. 'My godchild this' and 'my godchild that.'"

"Does she drink a lot?"

Debby didn't answer for a few moments, standing there on her wide brick, three-level porch. "I don't know," she finally said. "I don't

146

live there. All I know is that she wanted you to have a real good summer, made me promise to help you have a baaad D.C. good time. Do you say *baaad*—meaning great—in Chicago?"

"I really want to go back home."

"Willa, I can tell you what 'mean' is. I was looking forward to going to junior high school, couldn't wait. Mainly, I wanted to sign up for a sewing class. First I tried to get into an advanced sewing class. I couldn't do that because first you had to take something called Basic Sewing Techniques. First day, I was wearing a suit I made to show the teacher. She told me to take my seat, that the class was going to make aprons that day. She said she believed the sooner a student started sewing, the better. I made the apron. Perfectly. She hung up everybody's but mine. Then we had to make another apron. So—I bought a very difficult coat pattern—to impress her, so that maybe she could teach me some shortcuts or something. I cut out the coat and proceeded to sew. She kicked me out of class that day, just walked over to me and put me out—said I was undermining her authority. I wore the coat to school, and she passed me in the hall and didn't speak. Three times, I spoke to her. Now, that's *mean*!"

When Willa walked back into the house and locked the door for the night, she could hear Godmother's loud snoring. The sweetish smell of brandy seemed to fill the room, settling over her porcelain "children."

Willa walked quickly to the den, the room farthest away from her sleeping godmother, and called her mother in Chicago—collect. As soon as she heard her mother's voice, she started crying and telling her mother that she was homesick and that she wanted to come home. She didn't mention the brandy. Willa's mother told her that if she didn't feel any better about staying, then she could certainly come home—but "Give Bev a chance—you've been begging to go there for a long time."

"I met Debby."

"I see."

"She lives across the street."

"Good."

"She says 'yep' all the time. And, Mama, guess what?"

"What?"

"Debby sews. Debby makes everything she wears—even her slips!"

"Really?"

"Yep, for real. She sews like you."

"Great!"

"She's gonna teach me to sew some shorts."

"Uh, huh."

"For real, Mama."

"You want to sew, Willa Renee?"

"Yep! Just like Debby. I don't want anybody else to have clothes like me. I'm going to design my own—just like she does."

"Good for you."

"Mama, why did you let people call you 'Libba Lips' when you were a little girl? Godmother told me that's what they called you."

Willa's mother was silent on the phone for a while before she spoke. "That's just what people did then," she finally said.

"She wasn't your friend."

"Yes, she is."

"You don't have ugly lips!" Willa yelled, and didn't care if Godmother awoke and heard her. "Neither do I."

"We've got luscious African lips," Willa's mother said.

"We damned sure have," Willa said.

"Willa Renee!"

Willa and her mother were both laughing, and Willa felt better when she put the phone down. She had to be careful calling collect. Her mother did not have any money to waste on long-distance telephone calls.

After a long bath, Willa put on her favorite pajamas and lay down on the snazzy purple-flowered sheets. One long leg hung over the side of the bed and touched the woolen rug with the same purple-flowered design worked around the border. The soft rug felt good on her feet. The air conditioning was making her cold. Willa pulled the covers closer to her neck, but for some reason she kept her foot on the rug. People who are real tall can do this, Willa thought, and didn't really care if they could or not. The only thing that really mattered was the Godmother's hard, ugly words had been made distant by her mother's soft voice. Willa felt better. She pulled her leg back into bed, wrapped her arms around her fluffy pillow, and fell asleep. Then she was awakened by the sound of movement in her room.

Godmother was sitting at the vanity table. She was smoking a cigarette in the early morning light. "Go back to sleep," she said quietly—the brandy-voice all gone now.

"What's the matter?" Willa asked sleepily.

"Not one thing," Godmother answered.

Willa put her head back down on the pillow and lay without moving. She turned her head away from the acrid cigarette smoke. Cigarette smoke made her eyes water. Her eyes were already stinging.

"I like sitting in a bedroom at night watching a child I love sleeping. I've often wondered what it was like." Godmother's voice seemed even quieter.

Willa lay still, said nothing. She was looking out the window, past the trees, at the sky showing off its dawn colors. She felt free and outside of this room.

"When you've never had children, these things are missed. I'm enjoying sitting here. You dangled those long skinny legs off the bed, once or twice. I lifted them back onto the bed, as best I could, so as not to disturb you. Such skinny arms. As skinny as your mother's used to be. Angela never got fat like the rest of us. She's kept her girlish figure.

"My mother never had a lot of money to buy food," Willa said, and hated herself for speaking.

Godmother lit another cigarette. "Maybe not," she said. "Maybe she was never meant to be fat. I was fat as an infant and all throughout my life. Even when I was hungry and struggling to go to school and eating someone else's leftovers, I was fat. How do you like Debby? What did you two talk about?

"Nothing."

"Nothing?"

"We talked about sewing."

"Your mother could always sew. Oh, boy, could she sew. But she was always small and could buy clothes at any store."

Willa's eyes were watering badly.

"Angela was always drawing and reading and writing—poems. Sewing too—all the time. I can see her right now, seated at her mother's sewing machine, working the pedals. She would sit on the edge of the chair, those skinny legs just moving."

Willa listened.

"I lived with her family then. My mother was dead."

"Debby can make coats, Godmother."

"Would you like to make a coat?"

"No. She's going to teach me to make some denim shorts."

Willa turned over as Godmother put her cigarette out in an ashtray she held in her hand. Godmother left the room. "Go back to sleep," she said. "I didn't mean to wake you."

Later that morning, Willa helped Godmother work in her beautiful garden. They pulled weeds, trimmed some of the buds, cut flowers for the house, and watered the lawn. Willa was extra careful with her favorite flowers—the purple ones.

"Let's go," Godmother announced, as soon as the lawn was watered and lunch had been eaten and they had each taken another shower.

"May Debby go?" Willa had almost said "can" again.

"She may not. This is our time."

Willa was very surprised when Godmother opened the garage door and used her keys to get into a large station wagon. "I didn't know you could drive, Godmother. Why didn't you drive to the station to pick me up?"

"I detest that circle in front of Union Station. It confuses me. I never drive there."

"Oh."

"'Oh' is right. I've spent a fortune picking up people and paying taxicabs."

At the White Flint mall, Godmother looked at a directory of stores and headed upstairs on the escalator. Moments later, they entered a sewing machine shop.

"Why are we in here?" Willa asked, trying not to get excited, trying to stay calm.

"I haven't the slightest idea," Godmother said, sounding excited, too.

Godmother walked directly to a salesperson. "We want the nicest sewing machine, exactly what a 14-year-old would love to have."

Willa grabbed Godmother's arm. "Oh, my God!" she squealed. "Godmother, I was just going to use Debby's machine. Oh, my god! I can't sew!"

"You'll learn," Godmother said, "on your own machine. Your godmother's not a physician like Debby's daddy, but I think I can afford to buy my daughter a sewing machine."

Within an hour, Willa had a sewing machine with a zigzag stitch, a stretch stitch, an overlock stitch—and five other kinds of stitches. The salesperson taught Willa to thread the machine, fill a bobbin, select stitches, and adjust the tension—whatever tension was.

Willa sat in the back of the station wagon with her arm stretched over the top of the huge box containing what the salesperson called "a low-budget model." Willa thought her sewing machine was beautiful and fancy and just swell. Willa just kept thanking Godmother. Godmother laughed and kept driving. "I didn't want you to have to run over to Debby's house each time you felt like sewing."

As soon as the car stopped in front of the house, Willa jumped out of the car, leaving the huge box behind, and raced across the street to Debby. Both girls ran back to the car yelling, excited. Mr. Jesse Lee, a neighbor, lifted the sewing machine out of the car and took it up to Willa's room. He set up the machine, attaching it to a matching worktable. The girls were winding a bobbin before he got the box broken down and into the trash.

That night, brandy glass in her hand, Godmother said. "Now, Debby can come to your home to sew."

And Debby did. Godmother prepared all kinds of nice dinners and let them put on fashion shows—complete with music—when it was time to model the clothes the two girls had sewn. Willa taught Debby how to crochet and attach granny squares. Godmother played the piano and taught them how to make chocolate chip cookies from scratch.

Godmother made them laugh when she told them about some of her boyfriends. She made them sad when she told them of how relatives had put her out when once she couldn't afford to pay her weekly rent of three dollars.

"I was going to school and working as a nanny at the same time for one of the most successful Black doctors in town. I had absolutely no money to waste. Most of the time, I ate crackers and drank glasses and glasses of water. That particular day, I came home and found a cardboard box with my few clothes—and all my books—on the front steps. I called up to the window, but there was no answer from anyone inside. They were distant relatives and struggling as well, I suppose.

"I gathered up that box and walked and cried. I got on the bus with it and rode back to my job. The folks I worked for let me back in, let me live there, paid me less money, let me sleep in the basement in a room of my own. I began to eat decent meals. I was glad to be in that basement. That basement was all I had. I told myself that when I became a teacher, all of that would be forgotten. I did become a teacher—realizing my dream, but I never forgot the things that happened to me."

By the end of summer, Willa could sew. She had sewn three pairs of shorts, a pair for herself and a pair each for Marlena and Deanna. Each pair had scalloped edges but with three different kinds of fabric showing through: white eyelet lace, red plaid, and ruffled denim. Willa made matching blouses for the shorts, plain sleeveless shells. She had sewn Tommy a stuffed pillow made in the shape of a grand piano.

Then there was a surprise. The sewing machine wasn't really hers. Godmother wouldn't let her ship it home.

"The sewing machine stays here so you'll come back," Godmother said. "I hope you want to come back—next summer. You already have Angela's machine at home—and I've asked her if she would let you spend Thanksgiving and Christmas with me."

No way! Willa thought to herself. Well, maybe *part* of Christmas.

Two days before Willa was to leave, Godmother sipped more brandy and milk than usual. "I hope you weren't unhappy here," she said, sitting once again in Willa's room. It was three in the morning.

"I read one of Angela's letters to you, and I could see that you had told her something. I hope it wasn't too disparaging. Probably about my brandy."

Willa lay still.

"It must be nice to be able to write to a mother and tell her things. I wished many a day that I had had a mother to whom I could send letters. Actually, I wrote quite a few letters to my mother. The trick was to mail them. I couldn't mail them. The destination 'Heaven' doesn't work. No zip code."

"It's late, Godmother. Why don't you go to sleep?"

"I can sleep when you're gone."

"I know you're tired."

"I asked Angela what you needed for school. She said you didn't need anything. I found that amazing."

"I don't. I wear a uniform."

152

"Don't you need a new uniform?"

"No, Godmother. I wish you would go to bed and get some rest."

"You sleep. I'll just sit here."

Godmother told a few more stories about what it was like while she was growing up—but mostly, they were fragments of stories. Willa fell asleep trying to listen.

Later that day, Willa and Debby went to the Adams Morgan area to eat at the West Indian restaurant Wings and T'ings. "I want to buy Godmother a gift, but she has everything," Willa said. "Plus, I don't have much money left."

"I told you we should have sewn something for her," Debby fussed.

"But you didn't have any ideas about what to sew—and neither did I!"

It was while they were looking in an African shop that Willa saw exactly the present she wished to give her godmother. Willa prayed that she had enough money to buy the miniature figurine of an African woman dressed in kente cloth. There was another bit of cloth wrapped around a baby whose head was nestled against the woman's back.

Willa prayed harder.

"Do you love that?" the African merchant asked, his beautiful accent filling in the spaces around Willa, making her marvel.

"Yes," Willa said, and really meant it. "I hope it's not expensive."

"What is expensive?"

"Is it over five dollars?"

"Five dollar—exactly," the merchant said.

Both Willa and Debby stared at the doll. There was a small tag stating that the kente cloth was authentic. The name of the weaver was printed on the tag. The figures were so beautiful, and the faces were carved in an exquisite manner. The baby's face was no bigger than an eraser on a pencil. Both girls knew the cost had to be greater than five dollars. Willa picked up the tiny doll and held it close.

"Look at this," the merchant said, showing the wide-eyed girls a miniature box covered in the same kente cloth. "You must take them home in this."

Both girls asked in unison, "How much is that?"

"Since you have no more money," the merchant said, "it doesn't matter what the box costs. You cannot have one without the other."

On the way home, Willa and Debby worried about the package, didn't want to lose it. "Where's the package?" one or the other would ask whenever they stopped in a store to look at things.

"Suppose Godmother doesn't like it?" Willa asked Debby when they finally arrived home.

"We know she'll like it. Stop worrying."

"Godmother doesn't like Black books and art and stuff. She says 'a picture is a picture' and 'a book is a book.'"

Willa remembered the conversation.

"Your mother was always into Black this and Black that. It was Langston Hughes and Ann Petry and Henry Tanner. She knew them all. I liked Phillis Wheatley's poetry, but I was never into all that Black American–Black African stuff. I never started that sort of thing."

"My mother was always proud of being an African American. Daddy, too—that's what they taught us."

"Who said I'm not proud? And isn't it great that you had a mother and a father to teach you such things? I didn't."

Willa didn't feel like remembering. She felt like talking to Debby. "Thanks for seeing me through this summer," she said.

"There wasn't anything else to do," Debby said, grinning, "since neither of us knows Denzel Washington. Anyway, Ms. Beverly tells some wild stories, really weird. I like to hear them."

Willa stopped laughing. "Her stories are true," she said. "Not wild or weird."

"I would have run away if all that stuff happened to me," Debby insisted.

"If her mother hadn't died, all that 'stuff' wouldn't have happened to her. Besides, where would she run? She was already in the street."

"Time for me to go home," Debby said, and dashed across the street. "See you later, alligator."

"After while, crocodile," Willa said, and opened the door. There was the smell of brandy, and Godmother was snoring loudly from her bedroom. Willa went up to her beautiful bedroom and started packing her suitcase. In 24 hours she would be on her way to Chicago. Home.

Willa stopped packing and pulled out the miniature woman and baby. She placed the figures in the kente cloth box and wrapped

154

the box in purple wrapping paper she had bought from the drugstore. Then she tied the box with purple ribbon and placed a purple bow on top.

Where would she hide the gift? She didn't want Godmother to see it until after she, Willa, was gone. Willa decided that she would place the box on Godmother's dresser, next to the pictures of her parents, just before they left for National Airport. Godmother was treating her to a ride home on an airplane!

On this last night in Washington, D.C., Willa finished packing her suitcase, walked into Godmother's room, and sat down watching. Willa smoothed the woman's wispy hair, straightened the covers, and ignored the smell of brandy. Willa pushed the dark squat bottle against the antique white legs of the chest of drawers.

The glow from the night-light allowed Willa to see the photographs of Godmother's parents on the dresser. There were pictures of Godmother as an infant—all the way through her twelfth year, but no pictures after that of her childhood. There was her graduation picture from Coppin State College. She was wearing her black cap and gown. Deep dimples, the widest smile. Somehow she must have saved enough money to have her hair done at a beauty shop. The curls were shiny and neat beneath the tasseled mortarboard.

She looked lovely.

Godmother stirred in the bed, opened her eyes, and moved fitfully to the other side of the bed. "What are you doing in here? Go to bed."

"Just felt like talking, Aunt Beverly."

Godmother sat up, reached into the night table drawer, fetched a cigarette, lighted the tip, and drew the smoke in deeply. "Don't start that 'Aunt Beverly' again. It's time for you to go home—so go home."

"I am going home."

"Good. Now you can tell Angela everything I did wrong—and you won't have to wait and send it in a letter—as if she's the only one who knows what to do with children."

"She knows."

"Good for her."

"And so do you."

"Thank you, ma'am."

"Don't let the kids in your class call one another 'Libba Lips,' Godmother."

155

"Why are you so fixed on that? It wasn't all 'Libba Lips.' Angela—the angel—is what we called her most of the time. Skinny Angela. Skinny and lovely. She would never hurt anybody's feelings. She was shy, too shy. I was the big mouth."

"Godmother—"

"You should have seen your mother's notebooks. Her pictures of frogs looked better than the frogs in the book."

"I've seen Mama's notebooks."

"Then you saw that she got A's in everything."

"I know that."

"But she fell in love and had all those—"

"Babies."

"Yes."

"And you became Godmother."

"Yes—but just to you."

"You would love my brother Tommy," Willa said. "He plays the piano, and he's good at it."

"Tell him to be a music professor in a great conservatory, to play the piano so that people learn something—not just bang on it for fun."

"He doesn't 'bang' on it."

"Marvelous."

"He could really play that piano downstairs."

"Tell him come play it."

"Deanna is ahead of her class in math and is a math tutor. She didn't want to be skipped. She hopes to be a physicist. She registered for summer calculus classes. When I spoke to her last week, she said the classes were fun. She was sorry they were ending. She can't wait for school to start."

"Let's hope she doesn't fall in love right after high school and get married and have baby after baby after baby."

"Marlena draws like Mama and writes poems like Mama does—all day long. She wants to sculpt and attend law school and specialize in artists' rights."

"What about you?" Godmother asked. "Do you know what you want?"

Willa didn't answer right away. She watched Godmother blowing smoke into the air. Her eyes were stinging, tears were running down her face. The harsh smoke had nothing to do with her tears. Willa didn't really know why she was crying.

"I suppose you plan to be a designer and sew a million pairs of shorts—all of them looking exactly the same. God knows who would buy them—other than me."

"I want to be a schoolteacher. Like you."

"You don't want to be a teacher 'like' me, you want to be a *better* teacher than I am."

"I'll try."

"Don't just *try,* do it!"

"I may never get married, either."

"Don't be stupid, Willa."

"You didn't marry."

"I had suitors."

"You might have had a daughter."

"And die and leave her to people to put her out in the street."

"Godmother—"

"I have a daughter. You."

"I know."

"You've been my daughter since the day you were born."

Willa sat there in the dark until Godmother put her cigarette out and turned over and stopped talking. Willa didn't leave the room until she heard Godmother snoring again.

Back in her own room, Willa opened her suitcase and took out her purple writing paper. *Dear Godmother,* she began, *this note is for you. I hope you like my gift.* Willa wrote and wrote and wrote. She thanked Godmother for everything, mostly for the fun the two of them had shared.

A few hours later, Willa was back home in Chicago—hugging her mother, couldn't stop hugging her mother. She hugged Tommy and Marlena and Deanna too hard—each one. They were all laughing and talking at the same time. Tommy was glad to hear about the piano. Marlena and Deanna put on their short sets right away. Mama's gift was a blouse Willa had made. Mama was so proud of it.

"Teach me to sew like you," Willa pleaded.

Her mother hugged her. "We can start today."

Godmother had given Willa 100 dollars to help with school expenses. Tommy needed two new uniform shirts because he was

157

growing so fast. Willa bought the new shirts and everybody's school supplies.

On the first day of school, Willa received a letter from Godmother.

> Dearest Daughter:
> Thank you for the lovely African mother and daughter (of course, it's a girl) you left on my dresser. I think of it as the two of us. It has a place of honor, at the center of my mantel.
> The note you left did not have any unnecessary capital letters. I am proud of you.
>
> Love always,
Godmother
>
> P.S. Give my best to your family and thank God you have one.

The Fall

by Russell Edson

There was a man who found two leaves and came indoors holding them out saying to his parents that he was a tree.

To which they said then go into the yard and do not grow in the living-room as your roots may ruin the carpet.

He said I was fooling I am not a tree and he dropped his leaves.

But his parents said look it is fall.